# 100
# ACTIVITIES FOR DEVELOPING FLUENT READERS

## Patterns and Applications for Word Recognition, Fluency, and Comprehension

### SECOND EDITION

**Barbara J. Fox**
*North Carolina State University*

PEARSON

Merrill
Prentice Hall

Upper Saddle River, New Jersey
Columbus, Ohio

**Library of Congress Cataloging-in-Publication Data**

Fox, Barbara J.
  100 activities for developing fluent readers/Barbara J. Fox. —2nd ed.
    p. cm.
  Rev. ed. of Word recognition activities.
  ISBN 10: 0-13-156132-4, ISBN 13: 978-0-13-156132-8 (pbk.)  1. Word recognition.  2. Reading—Phonetic method.
  3. Reading (Elementary)  I. Fox, Barbara J. Word recognition activities.  II. Title.
III. Title: One hundred activities for developing fluent readers.
  LB1050.44.F69 2008
  372.46′5—dc22

                                        2007009437

**Vice President and Executive Publisher:** Jeffery W. Johnston
**Senior Editor:** Linda Ashe Bishop
**Senior Production Editor:** Mary M. Irvin
**Senior Editorial Assistant:** Laura Weaver
**Design Coordinator:** Diane C. Lorenzo
**Project Coordination:** GGS Book Services
**Cover Designer:** Candace Rowley
**Cover Image:** Artville
**Production Manager:** Pamela D. Bennett
**Director of Marketing:** David Gesell
**Marketing Manager:** Darcy Betts Prybella
**Marketing Coordinator:** Brian Mounts

The previous edition of this text was titled *Word Recognition Activities: Patterns and Strategies for Developing Fluency.*

This book was set in Palatino by GGS Book Services. It was printed and bound by Bind Rite Graphics. The cover was printed by Phoenix Color Corp.

Pearson Education Ltd.
Pearson Education Singapore Pte. Ltd.
Pearson Education Canada, Ltd.
Pearson Education–Japan

Pearson Education Australia Pty. Limited
Pearson Education North Asia Ltd.
Pearson Educación de Mexico, S.A. de C.V.
Pearson Education Malaysia Pte. Ltd.

10  9  8  7  6  5  4  3  2  1
ISBN-13: 978-0-13-156132-8
ISBN-10:    0-13-156132-4

# PREFACE

*100 Activities for Developing Fluent Readers: Patterns and Applications for Word Recognition, Fluency, and Comprehension* has classroom teaching activities for phonemic awareness, phonics, structural analysis, vocabulary, fluency, and comprehension. Since the National Reading Panel report in 2000, teaching the five components of learning to read has been on the minds of teachers, policymakers, and parents. Teaching the basics has always been part of the classroom reading program. Effective classroom reading programs teach the basics in an environment that stimulates and motivates children, offers children opportunities to develop literacy within the context of authentic, goal-oriented activities, creates opportunities for the child to think and act like a reader, and supports and facilitates reading for pleasure.

Instructional approaches have changed over the years and no doubt will continue to change and evolve. What does not change is the manner in which the child develops into a proficient reader. We have learned a great deal about how different components interact and affect one another as the child moves through the elementary program. Effective teachers use this knowledge to implement and sustain programs that maximize conditions for learning to read.

Fluency is in the limelight for the first time in recent memory. One would think that fluency is the new kid on the block from all the discussion. Fluency has been around for a long time; it was just not in such a prominent position as it is now. We teach fluency to support comprehension. The real goal is not so much an eloquent oral reader but, rather, an excellent comprehender. The decisions we make about what to teach, when to teach, and how to teach have a huge impact on the achievement of the children whom we teach. We need to make the right decision at the right time for the right child.

## AUDIENCE AND PURPOSE

This book is intended for teachers who are preparing to enter the classroom, teachers who are new to the classroom, and seasoned teachers who bring wisdom and experience to the classroom reading program. Its purpose is to offer preservice, new, and practicing teachers a resource to strengthen their classroom reading programs and, by extension, to improve the achievement of the children they teach. This book is not a laundry list of activities categorized by component. The activities in the book are nestled in text that informs you, the teacher, of the role these activities play in the learning-to-read process. You will learn how each of the five reading components uniquely contributes to literacy and how each component looks in the classroom, K–6. Each chapter also offers classroom-friendly, informal assessments to help you decide which children will benefit most from instruction using a particular activity.

## ORGANIZATION OF THE BOOK

This book is organized to maximize utility and minimize the time a busy teacher spends finding activities and locating information on informal assessment and best practices. The Introduction sets the stage for the chapters. It gives the reader a bird's-eye view of instruction as it contributes to fluency and comprehension. The introduction is followed by six chapters that are organized with a common, predictable format. Each begins with a brief explanation of how a reading component contributes to proficient reading, followed by a brief description of the component itself. Teaching activities are next. The purpose, grouping options, materials, and step-by-step directions make it easy to know whether a particular activity is suitable for the children whom you teach. The activities are followed by classroom-friendly, informal assessments. Chapters close with an explanation of how the component is integrated into classroom instruction. Highlighted in each chapter are best teaching practices, recommendations for teaching English language learners, and guidelines for working with children at risk.

The overriding goal of this text is to help each and every child learn to read and to have every child leave elementary school a confident, fluent reader who loves to read, who reads for pleasure, and who will use his or her reading ability to become a lifelong learner.

## ACKNOWLEDGMENTS

A special thank you to all the wonderfully talented teachers I have worked with over the years. Your assistance has been invaluable, your sage advice priceless; the commitment you bring to teaching is a credit to you and to our profession. This book could not have been written without your support and contributions.

This book is enriched by contributions of many teachers who used these activities in their classrooms and made suggestions for ways to make the activities more effective and easy to implement. These teachers also critiqued the activity sequence to ensure their use followed how fluency develops. I am very grateful for each of the specific contributions by Elizabeth Beecher, Heather M. Bosela, Malissa Bailey Carr, Krista Hockey, Ron Honeycutt, Allison J. Lewis, Vanessa Masterpolo, Kerry McCarthy, Mary Jane Mitchell, Zoa Murray, Kara Stewart, Krista R. Van Antwerp, Tamara R. Von Matt and Tonya Weitzel.

I also would like to thank the reviewers of my manuscript for their insights and thoughtful comments: Timothy Shanahan, University of Illinois at Chicago; Jane F. Rudden, Millersville University of Pennsylvania; Merry Boggs, Tarleton State University; and Ann A. Wolf, Gonzaga University.

# CONTENTS

# Chapter 3
# DECODING WITH STRUCTURAL ANALYSIS  63

# Chapter 4
# MEANING VOCABULARY  88

## Chapter 5
# ORAL READING FLUENCY 113

## Chapter 6
# COMPREHENSION 132

# INTRODUCTION

## HOW ACCOMPLISHED READING DEVELOPS AND UNFOLDS

Every teacher strives to develop fluent readers. Fluent readers are accomplished—they read with expression and with enough accuracy and at a sufficient pace to support comprehension. While these skills are essential, oral reading fluency is far more than just reading the words with speed and precision.

Fluent readers interpret text through their voices. They read in phrases and sentences and use punctuation to guide their voices. They also match their voices to meaning. Fluent readers are so proficient that we, the listeners, connect with text through the reader's voice. These readers use strategies to interpret text—they concentrate on meaning, monitor comprehension, and use fix-up strategies when comprehension breaks down. Fluent readers read more text, complete homework, and learn more with less effort and have higher achievement than nonfluent readers (Joshi, 2005).

Fluency develops in a logical, predictable way that begins when the preschooler imitates reading as she turns the pages of a storybook, cues on pictures, and tells a story that is consistent with the pictures. She often begins with "once upon a time" and "reads" with a smooth, conversational rhythm. The fluent, accomplished sixth grader also reads in a smooth, conversational cadence. Although the kindergartner and sixth grader differ widely in the skills and strategies they use, both have a model of fluency in their minds, both use that model to guide their reading, and both understand that comprehension is paramount.

Five learning areas come together in the elementary grades as children become readers. These five areas each make a unique contribution to the development of fluent reading and they are the teaching foci of this book. The five areas are phonemic awareness, word recognition (phonics and using multiletter parts in word structure to decode), vocabulary, fluency, and comprehension. Children begin their journey toward accomplished reading with an understanding of how fluent readers sound and should leave sixth grade with the ability to read text in the same smooth, expressive style they imitated in kindergarten. Good readers know that comprehension is key, and they do not lose their focus on meaning as they read. The difference between the kindergarten reader and the sixth grade reader is, of course, the level of text read and the knowledge each brings to the text.

Fluent, accomplished reading develops as follows: Phonemic awareness and phonics make it possible for the child to develop a large, rich, reading vocabulary. Reading vocabulary in turn makes it possible for the child to read fluently. Fluency opens the door to comprehension (Eldredge, 2005). Let us take a closer look at these components and how they interact as the child learns to read.

## Phonemic Awareness and Phonics Are Codependent

Phonemic awareness is the understanding that words consist of sounds. Phonics is the relationship between letters and sounds. These two skill sets are codependent when learning to read an alphabetic language like English. The reader needs some level of phonemic awareness to make sense of letter–sound relationships. In the other direction, using phonics while reading and spelling leads to better phonemic awareness.

*Phonics makes it possible to learn new words.* Our alphabet forms tens of thousands of words from just 26 letters. One of the downsides of a rather short list of letters is that many, many words look quite a bit alike. Many words have the same length, the same shape, and a lot of the same letters. For example, *short*, *shirt*, *shirk*, and *shark* differ by a single letter; *bat*, *bet*, *bit*, and *but* have the same shape and length. Yet the fluent reader does not read *short* for *shirt* or *bit* for *but*. The fluent, accomplished reader instantly recognizes a word by its spelling, knows its sound, and understands its meaning.

Learning to read English by sheer rote memory is nearly impossible. At the very best, memorizing each and every word as an intact unit—a gestalt—would take years and years. Our children do not need to do this. They have the alphabet to fall back on. The benefit of an alphabet is that it gives readers a shortcut to word learning. This said, the reader does learn a few words by sheer rote memory. The child reads and writes these words so often that he or she commits them to memory through repetition. The quickest way to learn words in an alphabet is to figure out pronunciation by associating letters, letter patterns, and multiletter word parts with sound.

A consequence of using phonics to learn new words is that spelling, sound, and meaning are bundled together in memory. Perhaps this explains why fluent readers are better decoders than nonfluent readers (Schwanenflugel, Hamilton, Kuhn, Wisenbaker, & Stahl, 2004). Because fluent readers are good decoders, they develop the ability to recognize words instantly, which brings us to the third component—vocabulary.

*Vocabulary and fluency are related.* The child's reading vocabulary consists of all the words the child instantly recognizes and understands. Fluent readers have the words on the tips of their tongues. Word recognition is fast, accurate, and effortless.

Although vocabulary and fluency are related to one another, they are not codependent. A rich and large reading vocabulary does not cause fluency. Efficient word recognition makes it possible to read fluently, to be sure, but vocabulary alone is not sufficient for fluency (Eldredge, 2005). The fluent reader brings to text a host of abilities and strategies that go beyond instant word recognition. The fluent reader understands how to use the voice to convey meaning, reads for a purpose, interprets meaning, critically evaluates text, and connects text to his or her own life, to name but a few processes and strategies.

*Fluency predicts reading achievement and opens the door to comprehension.* Fluency predicts the child's future reading achievement (Fuchs, Fuchs, Hosp, & Jenkins, 2001). We cannot say with certainty that fluency is the cause of reading achievement, but we can say that it is a critical factor in reading progress. Fluency may represent the child's ability to integrate the many comprehension processes and strategies in an efficient, effortless fashion.

Instantly recognizing words and understanding word meaning frees the mind to think about comprehension. All readers have a limited amount of attention. Attention that goes toward one task cannot be used to execute another. For example, you and I can pay attention to driving our car or we can stare at the fender bender on the side of the road, but we cannot do both at once. In order to shift attention away from driving our car to watching the fender bender we must compensate. Drivers do this by slowing down. Because their attention shifts to the fender bender, they intuitively know to back off the gas. The consequence is often a multiple-mile traffic jam.

Readers face the same dilemma. They can focus attention on comprehension or they can focus on word identification, but they cannot do both at once. Any attention that goes toward recognizing words is not available for understanding meaning. When the reader does not instantly recognize a word, the reader does the same thing we do when we approach a fender bender—the reader shifts attention away from comprehension and toward word recognition. Comprehension is now at risk. Every time the reader shifts attention to word recognition, comprehension is disrupted. If there are too many unfamiliar words, comprehension breaks down completely.

There is a reciprocal relationship between vocabulary and comprehension. As the child develops better comprehension, the child reads more difficult text. The more the child reads, the greater the likelihood that the child's reading vocabulary will increase. The greater the child's reading vocabulary, the greater the likelihood the child will read even more challenging text.

The reciprocal relationship between vocabulary and comprehension works to the advantage of the fluent reader, but it does not favor the nonfluent reader. Word recognition is not automatic for nonfluent readers. Nonfluent readers know fewer words. The child who knows fewer words spends less time reading. This child also learns words at a slower pace and has more difficulty understanding text than fluent readers (Harmon, Hedrick, & Wood, 2005; Joshi, 2005). Nonfluent readers need more direct instruction in vocabulary than their average-progress classmates (Cain, Oakill, & Lemmon, 2004).

*Fluency may vary when the child reads different types of text.* Fluency is somewhat specific to the type of text the child reads. A child who is a fluent reader of story text may not read her science book fluently. The reader needs to develop the ability to fluently read a variety of text. This means that we must help each child develop fluency in reading text across the curriculum.

*Fluency and automaticity are different.* The terms *automaticity* and *fluency* pepper teacher education classes, in-service education, journals, and textbooks. Sometimes one gets the impression that *fluency* and *automaticity* are synonyms. However, fluency and automaticity are not the same. Automatic tasks are done without conscious effort. Instant word recognition is automatic. We might think of instant recognition as a subroutine operating while the reader comprehends text. The wor d ecognition subroutine is essential for the larger process—comprehension.

Fluent reading is more than carrying out automatic word recognition. Readers intend to convey meaning. They interpret text through their voices. They perform for a listening audience. Consequently, the reader who is asked to read a short passage to a social group does not read without some amount of conscious effort. In fact, many readers rehearse before they read to the audience. Fluent reading calls on the reader to translate text into language that communicates with a listening audience. Automatic skills like instant word recognition support readers in this endeavor.

*Fluent reading in every grade.* The kindergarten child who does not yet recognize words successfully approximates fluent reading. The average-progress reader remains fluent at each grade by developing the tools, skill sets, and strategies that are necessary for reading grade-appropriate text. As the child's reading achievement increases, so, too, does the ability to read increasingly more difficult text with expression, accuracy, and an appropriate pace. Consequently, the average first grader reads first-grade text fluently; the average fifth grader reads fifth-grade text fluently.

*Fluency in your classroom reading program.* It is important for you to develop fluency in the children whom you teach. This said, fluency should not dominate your classroom reading program. The classroom program should make provision for teaching the skill sets and strategies that support and characterize proficient reading. Fluency is just one component. We want to provide instruction that is consistent with the child's development as a reader. If you use a structured, published program, you should, of course, follow that program. If you have a choice in the matter, spend more time developing the fluency of nonfluent readers. Give everyone opportunities to develop fluency and tie fluency-development lessons and experiences to other activities. For example, readers' theater develops fluency. Children could present a readers' theater play about a topic they are studying in social studies. Alternatively, children could repeatedly read in chorus the poems they are studying in language arts.

When all is said and done, accomplished, mature readers—say, readers finishing college—read and understand a variety of different texts, read for a variety of reasons, and enjoy reading for pleasure. They read fluently and confidently. Fluency in the elementary school years kept pace with the increases in reading ability that took place in each grade. At no time were these readers nonfluent. They entered into reading by imitating the fluent reading they heard in their classroom. They developed the skill sets to support word learning; they continually added words to their reading vocabulary; they understood the text they read. These readers and their teachers never lost sight of the goal of reading for meaning, reading fluently, reading to learn, and reading for pleasure.

Throughout elementary school, high school, and college, these learners read for pleasure in their spare time. They will continue reading for pleasure as adults. They have been and still are motivated learners. They left the elementary school with the strategies they needed to sustain them as readers. Their teacher at each grade made a significant contribution to their developing literacy. The cumulative effect of the efforts of their elementary teachers is a well-rounded citizen, a successful individual, and an adult who will read for pleasure for a lifetime.

## REFERENCES

Cain, K., Oakhill, J. V., & Lemmon, K. (2004). Individual differences in the inference of word meanings from context: The influence of reading comprehension, vocabulary knowledge, and memory capacity. *Journal of Educational Psychology, 96*, 671–681.

Eldredge, J. L. (2005). Foundations of fluency: An exploration. *Reading Psychology, 26*, 161–181.

Fuchs, L. S., Fuchs, D., Hosp, M. K., & Jenkins, J. R. (2001). Oral reading fluency as an indicator of reading competence: A theoretical, empirical, and historical analysis. *Scientific Studies of Reading, 5*, 239–256.

Harmon, J. M., Hedrick, W. B., & Wood, K. D. (2005). Research on vocabulary instruction in the content areas: Implications for struggling readers. *Reading and Writing Quarterly, 21*, 261–280.

Joshi, H. M. (2005). Vocabulary: A critical component of comprehension. *Reading and Writing Quarterly, 21*, 209–219.

Schwanenflugel, P. J., Hamilton, A. M., Kuhn, M. R., Wisenbaker, J. M., & Stahl, S. A. (2004). Becoming a fluent reader: Reading skill and prosodic features in the oral reading of young readers. *Journal of Educational Psychology, 96*, 119–129.

# 1

# PHONEMIC AWARENESS

Kindergartners sitting cross-legged on the classroom floor watch with rapt attention as Ms. Beecher holds up a cheery-faced puppet. They listen carefully as the puppet asks them questions, starting with, "What sound do you hear at the beginning of *mother* and *moon*?" "M," Susan replies. "How many sounds are in *cat*?" "Three," says Paul. "Say *stop* without the /s/." "Top," Paul shouts. "Start with *cat*. Add an /s/ to the end. What's the word?" "Cats," answers Tyrone. "What sounds do you hear in *fish*?" "F–i–sh," says Carlos. "What word does /p/–/a/–/n/ make?" Everyone says "pan" in chorus.

These kindergartners separate words into sounds and blend sounds together. They have good phonemic awareness and are well on their way to becoming good readers. *Phonemic awareness* is the understanding that each and every spoken word has one or more sounds (/me/ = /m/ and /e/), that those sounds can be pronounced separately (/m/–/e/), and when blended together the sounds form meaningful words (/m/ + /e/ = /me/).

When children develop phonemic awareness, they step away from word meaning and concentrate instead on small, meaningless sounds or phonemes. A *phoneme* is the smallest sound that makes one word different from another. For example, if we substitute the /a/ in /fat/ for an /i/, we pronounce a different word, /fit/. The /a/ and the /i/ are examples of two English phonemes. When we teach children to identify the beginning, middle, and ending sounds in words, and when we teach children how to blend, we are teaching phonemic awareness.

The four kindergartners demonstrated phonemic awareness when they quickly and easily answered the questions the puppet asked. Carlos demonstrated phonemic awareness when he separated *fish* into three phonemes: /f/–/i/–/sh/. Paul showed that he can delete sounds from words when he said /stop/ without the /s/. Everyone demonstrated blending when they combined /p/–/a/–/n/ into /pan/. These children are aware of the individual sounds in words. They think about the sounds individually, pronounce just one sound from a word, and blend sounds together. They understand that meaningful words consist of essentially meaningless sounds, and they use this knowledge when they sound out new words and when they associate sounds with letters to spell new words.

Phonemic awareness is a special kind of knowledge about spoken language that is different from speaking and listening. Phonemic awareness does not help children talk with you, their teacher, or with their friends on the playground. Children can be good conversationalists without phonemic awareness. Although children do not need phonemic awareness to use spoken language, they do need phonemic awareness to learn to read.

# PHONEMIC AWARENESS CONTRIBUTES TO VOCABULARY AND FLUENCY

Phonemic awareness is part of a chain of reading skills and abilities that contribute to fluent reading (explained in the Introduction). Phonemic awareness makes it possible for the child to use phonics to read and learn new words. Phonics is a key word learning strategy for children in kindergarten and first and second grade. Learning new words, in turn, results in a large and rich reading vocabulary. A large reading vocabulary is important because fluent reading hinges, in part, on instantly recognizing words (Eldredge, 2005). Fluent reading frees the mind to connect with meaning, to critically analyze text, and to take pleasure in reading.

Phonemic awareness develops early, in kindergarten and first and second grade. Although phonemic awareness is not necessary for carrying on everyday conversations, it is necessary for learning to read English. As a matter of fact, phonemic awareness is so crucial for success in learning to read that beginning readers with good phonemic awareness become good readers in first and second grade; children with poor phonemic awareness struggle with reading (Strattman & Hodson, 2005).

English, like all other languages written in an alphabet, uses only a small set of visual symbols, just 26 letters. Phonics is the systematic way in which the 26 letters represent sounds in spoken words and a way to teach the relationships among letters and sounds. In order to grasp the principle of alphabet writing, beginning readers must understand that words consist of sounds and that letters represent those sounds.

Once the beginning reader is aware of the sounds in words, the reader realizes that the letters in written words stand for sounds in spoken words. With this understanding,

## BEST PRACTICES FOR EFFECTIVE TEACHING

1. *Teach phonemic awareness early, directly, and systematically.* Children with good phonemic awareness in kindergarten are better readers in first and second grade than children with low awareness (Schatschneider, Fletcher, Francis, Carlson, & Foorman, 2004; Strattman & Hodson, 2005).

2. *Teach segmenting and blending.* Segmenting and blending are the most important phonemic awareness skills. Both are necessary for success in learning to read and spell (Ehri et al., 2001).

3. *Teach phonemic awareness in proportion to the child's needs.* Invest more time in teaching phonemic awareness to children with low awareness; move high-awareness children on to other reading and writing activities.

4. *Model how to use phonemic awareness while reading and spelling new words.* Whereas some children intuitively understand how to use phonemic awareness and phonics together, most need direct instruction. As you model, think aloud—explain why and how you use phonemic awareness—to make the process obvious to children.

5. *Teach phonemic awareness and phonics together.* Teaching phonemic awareness along with phonics is more effective than teaching phonemic awareness alone (Christensen & Bowey, 2005; Hatcher, Hulme, & Snowling, 2004; National Reading Panel, 2000).

6. *Teach small groups of children one or two phonemic awareness skills at a time.* Small groups give children more opportunities to respond and give you opportunities to observe the children who are and are not making adequate progress (National Reading Panel, 2000).

the reader grasps the idea that phonics is a tool for changing unfamiliar written words into familiar spoken words. Children use both phonemic awareness and phonics to learn new words. Phonemic awareness is a skill set that pertains to spoken language. Phonics is a skill set that pertains to the associations among letters (written language) and sounds (spoken language). These two skill sets are codependent. Children need some phonemic awareness in order to use phonics. Using phonics improves phonemic awareness.

Let us suppose that Connie, a beginning first grader, knows that /man/ has three sounds (/m/, /a/, and /n/) (phonemic awareness) and that *m* represents /m/, *a* represents /a/, and *n* represents /n/ (phonics). When she sees *man* for the first time, she knows that the letters in *man* represent the sounds in a word (phonemic awareness). She uses phonics to associate /m/ with *m*, /a/ with *a*, and /n/ with *n*. She uses the phonemic awareness skill of blending to combine /m/ + /a/ + /n/ into /man/. Connie uses phonemic awareness to make sense of phonics and phonics to identify and learn new words.

## RHYME AWARENESS AND PHONEMIC AWARENESS

The activities in this chapter develop rhyme awareness and the phonemic awareness skills of (1) identifying beginning sounds, (2) segmenting or separating words into individual sounds, and (3) blending individual sounds into words. We have not included rhyme awareness in our list of phonemic awareness skills because rhyme awareness calls for noticing bundles of sounds. Listening for several sounds is a less detailed analysis of spoken language than listening for individual sounds.

### Rhyme Awareness

Rhyme awareness can be a helpful jumping-off point for developing phonemic awareness for some beginning readers. Because identifying rhyme asks the child to listen for sounds inside words, it may introduce the child to the basic idea that a word can be divided into parts, albeit somewhat large sound parts. The letters that represent spoken rhymes are called rimes. *An* is an example of a written rime. The *an* in *man* and *pan* (the written rime) corresponds to the rhyming sound of /an/ in /man/ and /can/. Knowing the letters that represent beginning and rhyming sounds makes it possible for some children to read and spell words that contain these sounds. While rhyme awareness can be a helpful stepping-stone to phonemic awareness, it does not necessarily result in greater awareness of individual sounds (Macmillan, 2002), unless we teach children to identify the separate sounds in rhymes (/at/ = /a/–/t/) (Ehri & Robbins, 1992).

### Beginning-Sound Awareness

Beginning-sound awareness is the first real step toward becoming aware of all the sounds in words. Awareness of beginning sounds is less taxing than segmenting and blending and, therefore, is usually the first phonemic awareness skill children develop. Children who are aware of beginning sounds can identify the beginning sounds in words and identify words that begin alike. For instance, kindergartners who are aware of beginning sounds will tell you, their teacher, that /bat/ begins with a /b/, that /bat/ and /bug/ begin alike, and that /bat/ and /sit/ do not begin alike.

Rhyme awareness and beginning-sound awareness develop at about the same time (National Reading Panel, 2000). This makes sense when we consider how the child identifies rhyming words. In order to determine that /pig/ and /big/ rhyme, the child must isolate the rhyme from the other sounds in these words. In our example the child would separate the beginning sounds (/p/ and /b/) from the rhyme (/ig/). Consequently, the child who is aware of rhyming sounds is also aware of beginning sounds. The child who is aware of beginning sounds and knows letter–sound associations can use this knowledge along with picture clues and context clues to make an informed guess about a word's identity. For example, on seeing *moon* the child thinks of the sound *m* represents, looks at the picture for confirmatory clues, and thinks about meaning. This is the first step toward building a reading vocabulary through the use of phonemic awareness and phonics. You will be a more effective teacher when you encourage this practice. (See pages 19–21, "Informal Assessment or Additional Practices for Observing Developing Phonemic Awareness.")

## Segmenting

Segmenting and blending are the most important phonemic awareness skills. Segmenting is separating words into individual sounds (/pig/ consists of /p/, /i/, and /g/). Skill at segmenting develops in a predictable sequence. The child becomes aware of beginning sounds first (/pig/ begins with /p/), followed by awareness of ending sounds (/pig/ ends with /g/), and finally awareness of middle sounds (/i/ is the middle sound in /pig/). Identifying middle sounds is more difficult than identifying beginning and ending sounds. Consequently, the children in your classroom who are skilled at isolating beginning and ending sounds may need more practice to develop the skill of isolating middle sounds.

## Blending

Blending is combining sounds to form words, such as blending /s/ + /a/ + /t/ to pronounce /sat/. Children use blending when they sound out a new word. For instance, in sounding out *pan* the beginning reader first associates a sound with each letter (*p* = /p/, *a* = /a/, *n* = /n/) and then blends the sounds into a familiar word (/p/ + /a/ + /n/ = /pan/). Success at using phonics depends on blending the sounds together and, of course, on checking to make sure that *pan* makes sense in the reading context.

# ACTIVITIES

## 17 ACTIVITIES TO DEVELOP RHYME AWARENESS, BEGINNING SOUND AWARENESS, SEGMENTING, AND BLENDING

Now that you know which skills to develop, we will consider examples of activities for teaching rhyme awareness, beginning sound awareness, segmenting, and blending. These activities are most appropriate for small groups unless otherwise indicated. Combine activities with phonics and relate phonemic awareness to reading and spelling.

## 1.1   What's Missing from This Picture? Rhyme Clues for Completing an Unfinished Picture

- Small group
- Use to develop rhyme awareness.

The teacher gives children rhyming clues to help complete a partially sketched picture on the board (Figure 1–1).

**Materials:** Nothing special.

**Step-by-step directions:**

1. Sketch something on the board, omitting several important features (Figure 1–1). For example, you might draw a dog without a tail, eyes, and nose or a bicycle without handlebars, pedals, and just one wheel.

**Figure 1–1**
What's Missing from This Picture? Rhyme Clues for Completing an Unfinished Picture

2. Give children rhyming clues to the missing parts. If you draw a dog you might say, "Our dog needs something that rhymes with sail. What's missing?" Children say "tail" and you draw the tail. Continue saying "We need to add something to our dog that rhymes with rose." "Next comes something that rhymes with tie."

3. After completing the picture, you may wish to add accessories to the dog like a collar, leash, sweater, hat, or even sunglasses. Call on children who whisper in your ear what should be drawn next and give their classmates a rhyming clue for drawing.

## 1.2 Chants for Rhyming and Blending

- Small group
- Use to develop rhyme awareness and blending, and to connect sounds with letters.

Select a chant that best meets the needs of the children whom you teach.

**Material:** Nothing special.

**Step-by-step directions:**

### Rhyme Chant: use to develop rhyme awareness

1. Demonstrate the chant using four rhyming words. When children are familiar with the chant, invite individuals to think of rhyming words.

   Clap–Clap–Pat: <u>man</u>–Clap–Clap–Pat: <u>pan</u>
   Clap–Clap–Pat: <u>pan</u>–Clap–Clap–Pat: <u>fan</u>
   Clap–Clap–Pat: <u>fan</u>–Clap–Clap–Pat: <u>ran</u>
   Clap–Clap–Pat: <u>ran</u>–Clap–Clap–Pat: <u>tan</u>

### Blending Chants: use to develop blending and letter–sound knowledge

Children blend the beginning sound with ending or rhyming sounds.

### Blending Chant: Chant 1

I know a word.
It starts with /c/.

It ends with /at/.
What is the word?
/c/ /at/ makes /cat/!

Connect this chant with letters by writing letters on the board and pointing to them as children chant:

*c*

*at*

*cat*

### Blending Chant: Chant 2

I (clap) know (clap) a (slap) word (slap).
It (clap) starts (clap) with (slap) /t/ (slap).
It (clap) ends (clap) with (slap) /op/ (slap).
What (clap) is (clap) the (slap) word (slap)?
/t/ (clap) /op/ (clap) make (slap) /top/ (slap)!

### Blending Chant: Chant 3

This chant is more difficult because children blend each and every sound. Imagine yourself at a sporting event and you have a clear picture of the way this chant sounds. This chant works for short and long words.

Teacher: Give me an /f/          Children: /f/

Teacher: Give me an /a/          Children: /a/

Teacher: Give me an /n/          Children: /n/

Teacher: What's it say?          Children /fan/

Link sounds to letters by writing the following on the board.

*f*

*a*

*n*

*fan*

Begin with two-sound chants, such as /be/ or /no/, and then progress to three-sound chants: /run/, /nap/.

---

## 1.3      Show and Tell

- Pairs, individual, or learning center
- Use to develop rhyme awareness.

Children show items they bring from home and others in the class think of words that rhyme with the show-and-tell items.

**Material:** Small objects or pictures; paper sacks.

**Step-by-step directions:**

1. Children bring a small object or picture from home concealed in a paper sack. (Put a few objects in sacks for the children who do not bring sacks from home.) The objects stay hidden until you call on a child to show-and-tell the hidden object.

2. Children take turns showing an object (or a picture) while the group thinks of rhyming words.

3. You may wish to write rhyming words in a list on the board.

---

## 1.4     Engine–Car–Caboose

- Small group
- Use to develop segmenting.

Children use an engine, a car, and a caboose to identify the locations—first, middle, last—of sounds in words you pronounce (Figure 1–2). You can use any object or vehicle that has a distinct beginning, middle, and end.

**Material:** Poster board. Draw a picture of a train engine, a car, and a caboose on poster board (Figure 1–2).

**Step-by-step directions:**

1. Put three chairs side-by-side in a row in the front of the group. Ask three children to sit in the chairs. Give the child in the chair on the left the engine, the second child the car, and the third child the caboose.

2. The teacher pronounces a word with three sounds, such as /mat/, and then says one sound, /t/, perhaps. If the sound comes at the end, the child with the caboose stands up. The child with the engine stands for the first sound; the child with the caboose stands for the last sound.

3. Get everyone in the small group involved by giving each child a small engine, car, and caboose glued to popsicle sticks. Children listen for sounds and hold up the images to identify beginning, middle, or ending sounds.

4. Connect letters to sounds by asking volunteers to say (or find) the letters associated with the sounds.

**Figure 1–2**
Engine-Car-Caboose

*Children holding an engine, car, or caboose stand when they hear their teacher say a beginning, middle, or ending sound in a word.*

  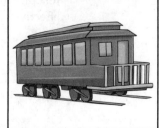

## 1.5    Sound Boxes with Pushing and Writing Letters

- Small group
- Use to develop segmenting and letter–sound knowledge.

Children develop phonemic awareness by pushing a token into a box for each sound heard. When boxes have letters that represent the sounds, children develop an understanding of the letter–sound relationships in words.

**Material:** Sound boxes, as shown in Figure 1–3; letter boxes, as shown in Figure 1–3; tokens; pictures with two-, three-, or four-sound names (optional). For letter pushing and letter writing you'll need blank boxes, small letters that fit in the boxes, and erasable markers.

**Step-by-step directions:**

### Sound Boxes—No Letters

1. Give each child a piece of paper with several groups of sound boxes. You may also wish to give children pictures to help them remember the words they are segmenting.
2. Stretch a word by elongating each sound while keeping the sounds joined together (/mmmaaannn/). Children push a token into a box for each sound heard. When children do not have much experience with sound boxes, pronounce words with easy-to-stretch beginning and ending sounds that you can say without interrupting airflow, as the /mmm/ and /nnn/ in /man/.
3. Once children have moved a token for each sound heard, ask them to point to the box that represents a single sound and to tell the sound's location—beginning, middle, end—in the word.
4. Have children blend sounds to pronounce the whole word, sweeping their fingers under boxes as they say the sounds.

### Letter Boxes

1. Give children letter boxes and say the word the letters spell.
2. Children point to each box as you say the sounds. If children already know some of the letter–sounds, have the children say the sound for the letters in the boxes.
3. Have children push chips into boxes for each sound heard.
4. Children remove the chips one by one. As each chip is removed, ask children to say the sound that goes with the letter.

### Pushing and Writing Letters

Joseph (2000) suggests taking boxes one step further. We find his suggestions quite effective.

**Figure 1–3**
Sound Boxes with Pushing and Writing
Letters

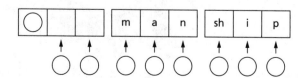

1. Use boxes with no letters. Begin by asking children to move a chip into each box for every sound heard in a word.
2. Then have children push letters into boxes for each sound heard.
3. Last children use erasable markers to write letters in the boxes.

## 1.6 Beginning-Sound Clothesline

- Small group
- Use to develop beginning-sound awareness.

Children use clothespins to hang words with the same beginning sounds on a clothesline.

**Material:** Construction paper; pictures; clothespins; rope. Beforehand, cut construction paper into clothes—pants, tops, dresses, skirts, shoes, caps. String the lightweight rope or heavy string across the classroom or zigzag it down a bulletin board, fastening it securely with thumbtacks.

**Step-by-step directions:**

**Figure 1–4**
Beginning Sound Clothesline

1. Show children several pictures. Put pictures in the chalk tray or on a table, depending on the size of the group with whom you are working. Have children find pictures that begin with the sound you specify. For example, you might ask children to find pictures that begin with /d/.
2. Give children construction paper clothes. Have children glue the pictures to the clothes. Alternatively, you might ask children to draw pictures rather than glue pictures on clothes.
3. Write the beginning letter above the picture on each clothing item.
4. Use clothespins to fasten the clothes to the clothesline, or the children might fasten the words to the clothesline if the bulletin board clothesline is accessible (Figure 1–4).
5. Read and reread the words in chorus. Point out beginning letters. Talk about how words that begin with the same sound also begin with the same letter.

## 1.7 Child-Created Beginning Letter–Sound Chants

- Small group
- Use to develop beginning-sound awareness

Children combine beginning-sound awareness with letter–sounds as they make their own chants.

**Material:** Colored markers or crayons; construction paper.

**Step-by-step directions:**

1. Write the same letter horizontally across the board, for example, *bbb*. Ask the children to name the letter and say its sound. Pronounce /b/–/b/–/b/. This forms the first part of the chant.

2. Ask children to think of a word that begins with the sound. For instance, children might think of *boat*. Sketch a boat.

3. Turn this into a chant by saying each /b/ in succession, while pointing to each letter, and then saying "boat." Have the group join you in chorus: "bbb boat."

4. Give each child construction paper and crayons. Have each child make three chants. Display the chants, and, at various times during the day, share the

**Figure 1–5a**
Child-Created Beginning Letter–Sound Chant

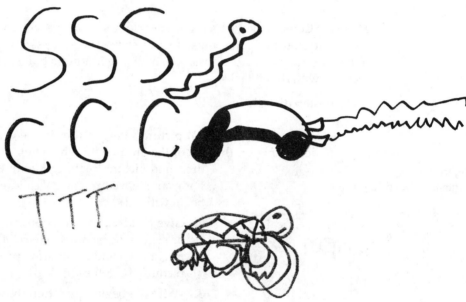

**Figure 1–5b**
Child-Created Beginning Letter–Sound Chant

chants with everyone in the class. Figures 1–5a and b show two groups of three chants each: (1) sss snake, ccc car, ttt turtle; (2) bbb bunny, ddd dragon, jjj jewel.

---

## 1.8    Stretching and Pulling Sounds

- Small group
- Use to develop segmenting and knowledge of letter–sound relationships.

Stretching and pulling are two complementary activities. Stretching gives children extra time to hear individual sounds in words. Pulling is a multimodal analog that calls attention to sounds and also connects sounds with letters.

**Material:** Nothing special for stretching sounds; short, decodable words (words that sound like they are spelled), such as *ham* or *sat*, for pulling sounds.

**Step-by-step directions:**

### Stretching Sounds

1. Pronounce a word, /*man*/, for instance. Say the word, elongating each sound, /mmmmaaaannnn/.
2. Stretch the word again. Write each letter on the board as you say the stretched sound. For example, you would write *m* as you say /mmmm/, *a* when you say /aaaa/, and *n* while pronouncing /nnnn/ to spell *man*.
3. Children join you in stretching /man/ in chorus, /mmmmaaaannnnn/, while you point to each letter as the sound is stretched.
4. Ask children to tell you the position of each sound. For instance, you might ask, "What's the beginning sound in *man*? The ending sound? The middle sound?"
5. Combine sound stretching with spelling for sounds (Activity 1.14).

**Figure 1–6**
Pulling Sounds

*A volunteer points to the letters on the board as the children pull and pronounce the sounds in /me/.*

### Pulling Sounds

1. Imagine that you are pulling a long string of bubble gum out of your mouth; only instead of gum you are pulling the sounds in words. Pull the sounds of a short word, such as /*me*/.
2. Ask the children to pull /me/ with you, together in chorus.
3. Once children can sound pull with you in chorus, have children stop when they pull /m/ and stop again when they pull /e/.
4. Write *me* on the board. Have a volunteer come to the board and point to the letters as the whole group pulls /me/ (Figure 1–6). Have the children join you in pulling the sounds.

### TEACHING ENGLISH LANGUAGE LEARNERS

1. *Teach phonemic awareness to English learners the same way you teach English-only children.* English learners and English-only children develop phonemic awareness in a similar fashion (Chiappe, Siegel, & Wade-Woolley, 2002). Although no special materials are necessary, you may need to spend more time teaching phonemic awareness, depending on children's ability to speak English and their development as readers.

2. *Use phonemic awareness activities to help develop awareness of English sounds and to give children practice saying English sounds.* Phonemic awareness activities draw children's attention to English sounds (Birch, 2002). Asking "Which words end alike? /cat/ /sit/ /mouse/?" gives English learners opportunities to learn which sounds belong in English. Asking "What sound do you hear at the beginning of /mouse/?" gives children practice pronouncing English sounds.

3. *Try to develop phonemic awareness in the children's home language first.* Developing phonemic awareness in the children's home language first facilitates developing phonemic awareness in English (Lefstedt & Gerber, 2005; Manis, Lindsey, & Bailey, 2004; Quiroga, Lemos-Britton, Mostafapout, Abbott, & Berniger, 2002).

4. *Use manipulatives—objects children touch, hold and move—to make English sounds more noticeable and obvious.* Because sounds disappear rapidly, grasping sounds can be difficult for English learners. Objects like plastic letters remind children of the sounds, which in turn makes it easier for English learners to develop phonemic awareness.

## 1.9    Sorting Sounds

- Learning center
- Use to develop awareness of beginning sounds, ending sounds, or middle sounds.

Children pronounce picture names and sort for shared sounds.

**Material:** Pictures.

**Figure 1–7**
Sorting for Beginning, Middle, or Ending Sounds

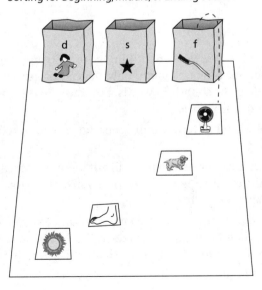

**Figure 1–8**
Sorting for the Number of Sounds in Words

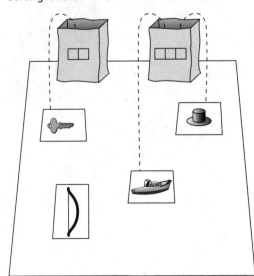

**Step-by-step directions:**

1. Place pictures and small sacks with pictures that represent the same speech sounds in the beginning, middle, or ending position in a learning center, as shown in Figure 1–7.

2. Pairs work together to sort pictures into groups that share the same beginning, middle, or ending sounds into sacks placed in a learning center.

3. An alternative is to draw connected boxes on sacks to represent the number of sounds in picture names (Figure 1–8) and ask children to sort pictures according to the number of sounds in the picture names.

---

## 1.10    Letter–Sound Cubes

- Small group
- Use to develop beginning-sound awareness.

Children toss a cube with a picture and a letter on each side, and think of words that begin with the same sound (Figure 1–9).

**Material:** Cubes with letters or cubes with letters and pictures. Figure 1–10 illustrates how to make a cube. Fold on the dotted lines and tape the cube together.

**Step-by-step directions:**

1. Children in a small group take turns tossing the cube.

2. Children say a sound associated with the picture and the accompanying letter and then say another word that begins with the same sound.

3. Write the words. Underline or point out the beginning letter. Talk about beginning sounds and letters.

4. For a more challenging activity, have children toss cubes with a single letter (no picture) on each side. Follow the same procedure.

**Figure 1–9**
Letter–Sound Cube

*Directions: Have a small group of children take turns tossing the cube. Children say a word that begins with the same sound as the face-up picture and the sound associated with the letter and think of another word that begins with the same letter-sound.*

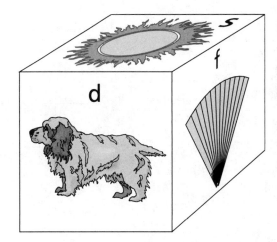

**Figure 1–10**
Cube Pattern

*Directions: Enlarge the pattern. Fold where you see dotted lines. Tape the cube together.*

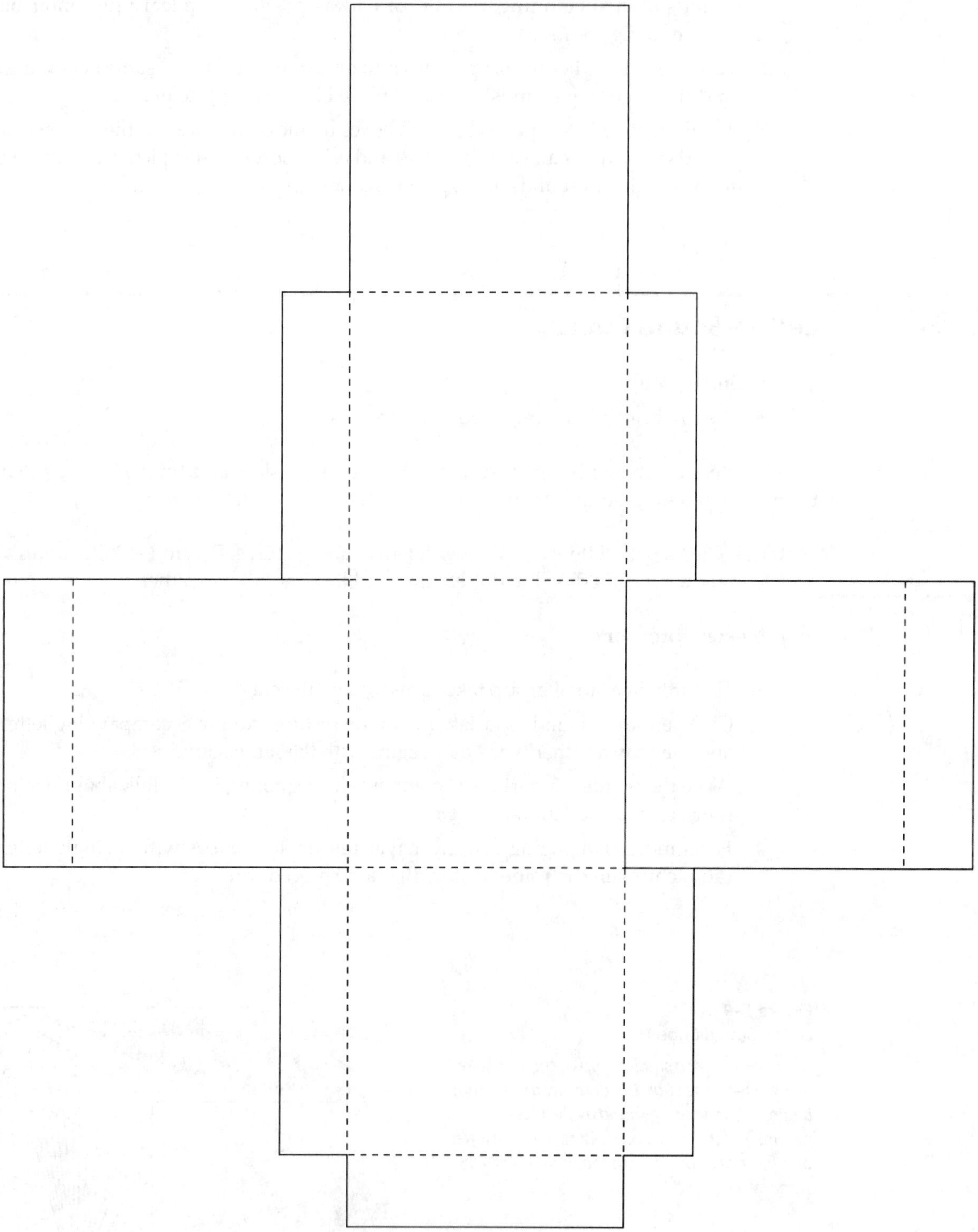

## 1.11 Beginning-Sound Bag Game for Pairs

- Pairs, learning center
- Use to develop beginning-sound awareness.

Lewkowicz (1994) suggests this sound game for pairs. The interactive game works well in a learning center when you have reviewed the objects used in the game with the children before they visit the center.

**Material:** Paper bags; several pairs of objects or pictures that begin with the same sound.

**Step-by-step directions:**

1. When children are familiar with the pictures or objects, place pairs of pictures (or objects) that begin with the same sound in each bag. For instance, pictures of a fan, shell, sun, ball and mop would go into one bag. Pictures of a fish, shoe, soap, bird and moon would go into another bag.
2. Each child has a bag. One child takes an object or picture out of the bag. The other child says the object or picture name.
3. The second child looks in his or her bag to find an object that begins with the same sound. The child takes the object out of the bag.
4. Children take turns until the bags are empty.

## 1.12 Loud Voice–Soft Voice

- Small group
- Use to develop beginning-sound awareness, ending-sound awareness, and knowledge of letter–sound relationships.

This activity is an easy and effective way of calling children's attention to beginning sounds and to the consonants that represent those sounds. It may also be used to call attention to ending sounds after children are aware of the first sound in short words.

**Material:** Pictures that begin or end with the sounds children segment from words; letters to represent the sounds; an alphabet strip for each child.

**Step-by-step directions:**

1. Show children a picture of a word that begins with the sound children will segment, for example, *sun*. Show children the picture and say its name, /sun/. Show children the letter *s*. Explain that we use the letter *s* to represent the /s/ in /sun/. As you pronounce the /s/, stretch it to make the sound more obvious, /ssssun/.
2. Have children say /sun/. Ask children to listen to the first sound /ssss/ in /sun/. Have children say /ssssun/ twice: /ssssun/ /ssssun/.
3. Ask children to say /ssss/ in a loud voice and to whisper /un/ in a soft voice. This might sound like: /**ssss**–un/. Ask children to do this two or three times: /**ssss**–un/ /**ssss**–un/ /**ssss**–un/.
4. Remind children that the *s* represents /**ssss**/. Have children point to the *s* on their alphabet strips. (If children do not have individual alphabet strips, ask a volunteer to point to the letter *s* you are using to demonstrate.)

5. Talk about other /ssss/ words. Find words on the word wall. Have children suggest other /ssss/ words. Write them on the board; add some to the word wall.

6. On future occasions have children continue to pronounce the first sound in other words in a loud voice /**mmmm**/ and the rest of the word in a soft voice /**mmmm**–an/. Consonants where we interrupt airflow, such as /b/, /p/ or /d/, cannot be stretched. Pronounce these sounds in a lively, quick staccato: /**b,b,b,b**–in/.

7. Later switch to ending sounds, for example, /ca–**nnnn**/.

8. Gradually you will be able to simply ask children to say the first or last sound; no soft voice–loud voice will be necessary.

---

## 1.13　Blending Slide

- Small group
- Use to develop blending and letter–sound knowledge.

A picture of a playground slide helps children visualize the blending process and guides them as they blend.

**Material:** Picture of a slide (Figure 1–11a); a small construction paper mouse for each child in a small group.

**Step-by-step directions:**

1. Draw a slide on the board. Explain that we slide sounds together as we blend. Write the letters of a word from the top to the bottom of the slide (Figure 1–11b).

**Figure 1–11b**
Mouse Blending

*Children practice blending when they "slide" a construction paper mouse down a slide while blending sounds together.*

**Figure 1–11a**
Blending Slide

2. To blend /fat/, put your hand on the top of the slide when you pronounce /f/, in the middle of the slide when you say /a/, and toward the bottom as you pronounce /t/. Beginning at the top of the slide, blend the /f/, /a/, and /t/ together as you slide your hand to the bottom. Pronounce /fat/ when you reach the bottom. Have children join in blending; invite individuals to be the "slider."

### Mouse Blending

1. Give each child a piece of paper with a picture of a slide (Figure 1–11b) and a construction paper mouse that is small enough to "slide" down the blending slide.

2. Pronounce another three-sound word, such as /fan/. Have the children identify the beginning, middle, and ending sounds. Write the letters that represent these sounds in the appropriate place on the slide you have drawn on the board. Demonstrate blending /fan/ (/f/ /a/ /n/), following the procedure you used when blending /fat/.

3. Children use the small mice to "slide" down the blending slide as everyone blends, in chorus, /f/, /a/, and /n/. Repeat with other words.

---

## 1.14   Spelling for Sounds

- Small group
- Use to develop segmenting and letter–sound knowledge.

In spelling for sounds the children join you in spelling a word by associating letters with sounds.

**Material:** Chalk- or whiteboard; chalk or dry-erase markers. Decodable words (words that are spelled as they sound).

**Step-by-step directions:**

1. Select a word children want to spell or wish to include in a group-composed story. For instance, in order to spell *sad*, you would sound stretch /sad/—/ssssaaaad/—and ask children to listen for the first sound.

2. When children say the sound, in this example /s/, ask them to name the letter that the /ssss/ represents, and write *s* on the board.

3. Stretch the second sound, /saaaaaaa/. Ask children to identify the letter that represents the sound. Write *a* beside *s*. The writing now looks like this: *sa*.

4. We cannot stretch /d/ for a long period because the airflow is obstructed while saying this sound. Instead of stretching the sound, pronounce the /d/ with a strong voice emphasis so as to draw children's attention to this sound: /ssssaaaa**d**/ or repeat the sound several times /ssssaaaa**d,d,d,d**/. Children say the sound that /d/ represents, thus completing the spelling of *sad*.

If the children in a small group do not yet know all the letter–sounds, assist them by writing in the letters for sounds they have not yet learned.

## 1.15   Grab Bag Blending

- Small group
- Use to develop blending.

Children guess a hidden object or picture by blending sounds into words.

**Material:** Paper sack; small objects or pictures.

**Step-by-step directions:**

1. Put small objects or pictures in a bag; keep the objects or pictures hidden.
2. Grab an object or picture; pronounce each sound. For instance, you might say, "This is a /c/, /ow/ or this is a /c/ /a/ /t/. What is it?"
3. Children guess the object or picture by listening to the sounds and blending them into a word.
4. Give additional hints to children who need extra help by stretching the word and then pronouncing its sounds in isolation.

## 1.16   What Am I?

- Small group
- Use to develop segmenting.

Children play a guessing game by changing one beginning sound for another in order to figure out the identity of hidden objects or picture. This game is more difficult and a logical follow-up for Grab Bag Blending. Use What Am I? with children who have some ability to blend and who are learning to manipulate sounds in words.

**Material:** Pictures or small objects.

**Step-by-step directions:**

1. Hide something behind your back such as a pen.
2. Say, "I have a /shen/. Take away the /sh/ and add a /p/. What is it?"
3. When children say /pen/, show them the pen. Ask individuals to whisper in your ear suggestions for something to hide.

## 1.17   Arm and Finger Blending

- Small group
- Use to develop blending.

In these two multimodal versions of blending, children use their arms or fingers to anchor sounds in memory and to guide blending.

**Material:** Nothing special.

**Step-by-step directions:**

### Arm Blending

1. Show children how to "place" a beginning sound, such as the /m/ in /mat/, by touching the shoulder.
2. Place the middle sound, the /a/, on the elbow and the /t/ on the wrist. Place the imaginary sounds on the arm that is opposite of the child's preferred hand.
3. Children blend by saying sounds as they move their hand from their shoulder to wrist. The fluid sweeping motion from shoulder to wrist encourages children to blend the sounds together in a natural flow.

### Finger Blending

1. For the purposes of illustration, let's suppose that children are blending /l/, /a/, /m/, /p/ into /lamp/. Children touch their forefinger to their thumb while saying /l/, their middle finger to the thumb saying /a/, their ring finger to the thumb while saying /m/, and their little finger to the thumb saying /p/.
2. To blend, children rapidly touch each finger to the thumb as they pronounce sounds, thereby blending sounds into /lamp/.

---

## INFORMAL ASSESSMENT OR ADDITIONAL PRACTICES FOR OBSERVING AND DEVELOPING PHONEMIC AWARENESS

### Additional Practices

*Shared reading.* Shared reading is a teaching practice in which the teacher provides scaffolding for beginning readers as a small group listens to the teacher read a big book and then rereads portions of the text. During shared reading we have many opportunities to call children's attention to the sounds in words and the letters that represent those sounds. Follow these steps:

1. Introduce the book. Point out and discuss the title and author. Take a picture walk through the book. A picture walk is a means of previewing the story by looking at the pictures and discussing characters and events.
2. Relate children's background experiences to the story. Set a purpose for reading.
3. Read the book at least once, maybe more if time permits. Point to the words as you read them.
4. The next day, read and reread the book. Have the children join in the reading. The group reads in chorus followed by individual children reading short portions. The teacher fills in the words that children do not know or cannot remember.
5. Select a beginning letter and sound to emphasize. Have children find words in the text that begin with the letter–sound. Review other letters if time permits.
6. Follow up by making lists of words with the same beginning letter-sound. Read the lists together in chorus. Have children read little versions of the big book with a partner and individually. If possible, send the small book home so child can share his or her emerging literacy with the family.

*Alphabet books.* As you share alphabet books have children find pictures that begin with the featured sounds and say the sounds at the beginning of picture names. Make alphabet books, too. Have children make pages for the letters they are learning. Individuals or pairs make pages on colorful construction paper or the whole group might make a book together. Use chart paper for the pages of a group-made alphabet book.

*Tracing and blending.* Tracing and blending develop phonemic awareness and link spoken sounds to the letters in the words children trace. Children trace letters as they pronounce the sounds. For example, if children are learning the word *an*, they would trace *a* while saying /aaa/ and *n* while saying /nnn/. Have children stretch the sounds so that the sounds fold into each other: /aaaannn/. The tracing finger helps guide the voice and looking at the letters helps make sounds more obvious and anchor them in memory.

*Line-up activities.* Ask children to line up in response to:

1. "Get in line if your name begins with the first sound in *bug*."
2. "Line up if your name ends with the last sound in *class*."
3. "Stand in line if your name has the middle sound in *pat*."

*Share poetry and find rhyming words.* Read and share rhyming poems and jingles. Ask children to join you repeating familiar rhymes in chorus. Sweep your hand under the words as they are read. When children are familiar with the poem, cover two or three rhyming words with sticky notes. Pause at each sticky note while reading the poem. Ask children to tell the rhyming words the sticky notes cover. Remove the sticky note once children say each rhyming word. For instance, in "Jack and Jill" you would pause at *hill*—"Jack and Jill ran up the _____"—and children would say "hill." Point out written words that represent the rhyme. In our example, the rhyme (the /ill/ in Jill and hill) corresponds to the rime *ill*. Sometimes rhyming sounds do not correspond to the same letters. *Head* and *bed* rhyme but the rhyming sound is not spelled alike. Look for words in which the spoken rhyme (/ill/) corresponds to the same written rime (*Jill, hill, pill, fill*).

## Informal Assessment in the Classroom

Children show us they have developed a particular skill when they apply it in the classroom. For example, answers to the questions you would normally ask during instruction reveal the child's awareness of rhyme and beginning sounds and the child's ability to segment and blend. Use questions like the following to teach and assess simultaneously.

*Rhyme awareness*

- "Do *big* and *pig* rhyme?"
- "Which one doesn't belong: *sock, man, rock*?"
- "Say a word that rhymes with *can*." "*Can, ran.* What's another rhyming word?"

*Beginning sound awareness*

- "What does *mouse* begin with?" "What's the first sound in *monkey*?"
- "Do *mop* and *moon* begin with the same sound? What's the sound?"

*Segmenting*

- "What sounds do you hear in *toad*?"
- "Say all the sounds in *soap*."

*Blending*

- "What word is this: /m/ /e/?"
- "What word do we get when we blend together /h/ /a/ /m/?"

Children also demonstrate rhyme and beginning-sound awareness and skill at segmenting and blending as they participate in the activities in this chapter. For example, as children participate in Activities 1.1 (What's Missing from This Picture?) and 1.3 (Show and Tell), you will be able to judge their ability to rhyme. As children participate in Activities 1.7 (Child-Created Beginning Letter–Sound Chants), 1.9 (Sorting Sounds), 1.10 (Letter–Sound Cubes), and Activity 1.11 (Beginning-Sound Bag Game), you will be able to observe their competence at identifying beginning sounds. Children identify individual sounds in Activities 1.4 (Engine–Car–Caboose), 1.5 (Sound Boxes with Pushing and Writing Letters), and 1.9 (Sorting Sounds). Children demonstrate blending ability as they participate in Activities 1.13 (Blending Slide), 1.15 (Grab Bag Blending), 1.16 (What Am I?), and 1.17 (Arm and Finger Blending). Children who segment and blend successfully without copying their neighbors or help from you are ready to move on. Children who wait for guidance need more instruction and guided practice.

*Counting and tapping.* Have children count the sounds in a word or tap once for each sound heard. This not only gives children practice listening for sounds but also gives you valuable information about the child's ability to identify the individual sounds in words.

## PHONEMIC AWARENESS IN THE CLASSROOM

### Kindergarten

Phonemic awareness receives the most emphasis in kindergarten and beginning first grade. Kindergartners learn to identify and think of rhyme, if they have not developed rhyme awareness in preschool. Children learn to segment two- or three-sound words into sounds and learn to blend two or three sounds into words. Teachers set aside at least 30 minutes or more for word study, which consists of teaching phonemic awareness, letter names, a sound for each letter, word families (<u>c</u>at, <u>b</u>at, <u>h</u>at, <u>r</u>at), and high-frequency words. Phonemic awareness is integrated into ongoing classroom instruction, so kindergartners actually receive more instruction than that provided during the 30 minutes of word study.

**Figure 1–12**
Brandon's Story

Brandon (Figure 1–12) and Kevin (Figure 1–13) are in the same kindergarten classroom. Brandon copies print from his classroom—in this instance, the alphabet his teacher taped to the wall. He knows that letters are important, but he does not understand how letters represent sounds. In Brandon's story letters do not correspond to sounds, so his kindergarten teacher cannot read what he writes. Interestingly, when Brandon's teacher asks him to read his story, he tells what he wrote immediately after writing. After a few hours or the next day, however, Brandon has forgotten what he wrote and cannot read his story. Since white spaces do not serve any real function from Brandon's point of view, he ignores them in writing. Yet Brandon realizes that writing is meaningful and that writing has letters.

**Figure 1–13**
Kevin's Story

The teacher knows that Brandon will benefit from learning to identify rhyme and beginning sounds. Therefore, the teacher encourages Brandon to identify beginning sounds and to associate letters with these sounds through such activities as reading alphabet books, making charts of begin-alike words, and calling attention to beginning letter–sounds during shared reading, as well as Activities 1.6 (Beginning-Sound Clothesline), 1.7 (Child-Created Beginning Letter–Sound Chants), and 1.10 (Letter–Sound Cubes). Activity 1.9 (Sorting Sounds) develops beginning-sound awareness when the child is asked to sort picture words according to beginning sounds; Activity 1.12 (Loud Voice—Soft Voice) develops beginning-sound awareness when the child says the beginning sound in a loud voice and whispers ending sounds (/ssssun/).

Kevin is further along in developing phonemic awareness and learning to read. Kevin remembers some words by sight. When Kevin reads easy books he first looks for pictures to help him figure out new words. If he sees a picture that makes sense in the story, he says the picture name. Kevin may also choose to look at the beginning letter–sound and, sometimes, the ending letter–sound. Since Kevin can already segment beginning and ending sounds, and knows a sound for each letter, his teacher focuses on separating the middle sounds in words and encourages him to read and spell new words by referring to the context and associating sounds with all the letters—beginning, middle, ending in short words like pan. Though many kindergartners will not reach the level of awareness we see in Kevin, all kindergartners benefit from a combination of phonemic awareness and letter–sound instruction appropriate to each child's needs.

Kevin's teacher uses Activities 1.4 (Engine–Car–Caboose), 1.5 (Sound Boxes with Pushing and Writing and Letters), 1.8 (Stretching and Pulling Sounds), and Counting and Tapping to further develop Kevin's ability to identify the sounds in words. Activity 1.9 (Sorting Sounds) is also useful, provided that Kevin sorts for ending or middle sounds. Because blending is a necessary skill, his teacher uses Activity 1.13 (Blending Slide), Activity 1.15 (Grab Bag Blending), and Activity 1.17 (Arm and Finger Blending) to develop blending. The teacher also uses Activity 1.14 (Spelling for Sounds) when Kevin participates in a group story writing activity in which the children suggest text and the teacher scaffolds writing by helping children with words they cannot spell.

## First Grade

Most average first graders begin the year with some ability to segment and blend short words. First-grade teachers build on this foundation, with the expectation that by the end of the year children will be skilled at segmenting and blending. In the beginning of the year, phonemic awareness is usually taught every day in connection with phonics. After a few weeks, phonemic awareness is taught just three or four times a week, depending on children's development as readers. Toward the middle or slightly after midyear, phonemic awareness is taught only twice a week, usually at the beginning of the week when letter–sound associations are introduced or reviewed.

Kelly (Figure 1–14) is aware of the sounds in words, as we see from the manner in which she spelled *because* (spelled *be kuzs* and *be cus*). She wrote this story during the second month of school, which reads: "I like my dog because it is the cutest dog I've seen on earth." Kelly conventionally spells *I, my, dog* (with a reversed *b/d*), *it, is, the,* and *on*. These words are in Kelly's reading vocabulary.

## WORKING WITH CHILDREN AT RISK

1. *Identify children with poor phonemic awareness early.* Poor phonemic awareness in kindergarten is a sign that the child is at risk for reading difficulty in later grades (Schatschneider, Fletcher, Francis, Carlson, & Foorman, 2004); Torgesen, 2002).

2. *Set aside extra time to teach phonemic awareness in kindergarten and first grade.* Because at-risk children are slower to develop phonemic awareness than average readers, reserve extra time to develop the phonemic awareness of these children.

3. *Put the most effort into developing phonemic awareness, not rhyme awareness.* Teaching phonemic awareness and phonics to at-risk children is more effective than a sole focus on beginning sounds and rhymes (Hindson, Byrne, Fielding-Barnsley, Newman, Hine, & Shankweiler, 2005; Yeh, 2003).

4. *Make segmenting as easy as possible.* Segmenting is easier when a vowel precedes a consonant (/in/, /at/) and is somewhat more difficult when a consonant precedes a vowel (/ma/, /ta/). When children are comfortable segmenting these two-sound combinations (/in/, /ta/), ask them to segment short, three-sound words (/sit/) (Geudens, Dominiek, & Van den Broeck, 2004).

5. *Make blending as easy as possible.* Teach children to blend a beginning consonant and a vowel with the last sound (/sa/ + /t/ = /sat/) (Cassady & Smith, 2004). Next teach children to blend the beginning sound /s/ with the sounds that follow (/s/ + /at/ = /sat/). When children are comfortable blending the beginning sounds and the remaining sounds, teach them to blend single sounds (/s/ + /a/ + /t/ = /sat/). This is the hardest form of blending.

6. *Teach children to blend stretchable sounds.* The sounds we pronounce until we run out of breath are easier to blend than sounds that abruptly stop. Begin with stretchable sounds (/sss/, /mmm/); these sounds are easier to blend than sounds we cannot stretch.

She sounds out new words by paying attention to the beginning, middle, and ending letter–sounds. She spells known words conventionally and invents ways to spell other words. She invents her own unique spellings by saying words to herself, listening for all the sounds in words, associating a letter with each sound, and then writing the letters. As a consequence, Kelly spells words the way they sound, not necessarily the

**Figure 1–14**
Kelly's Story

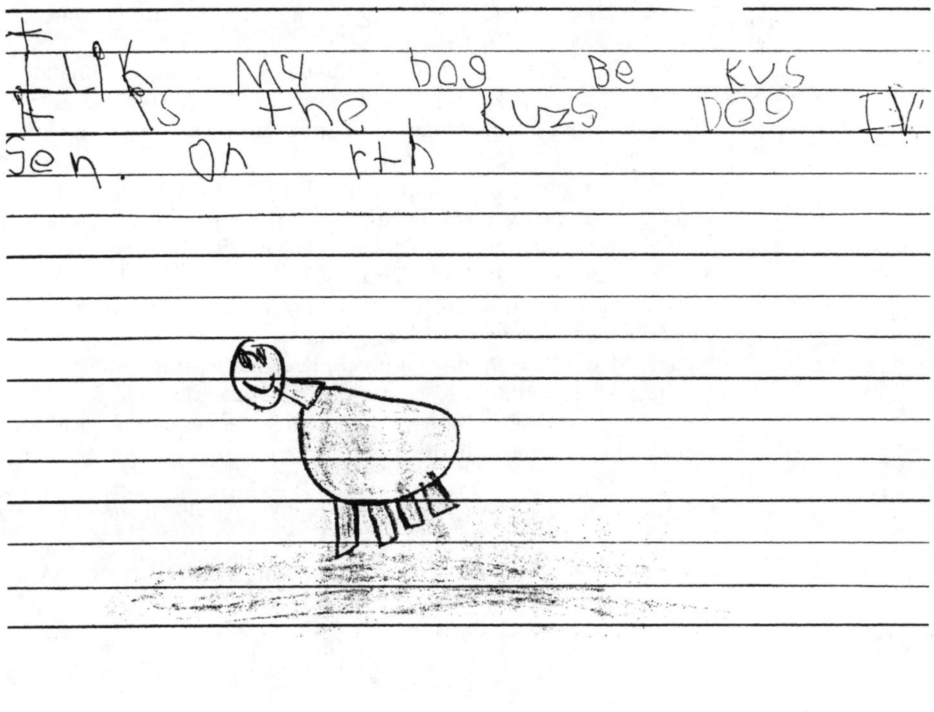

way they look. For example, she spells *seen* as *sen* and *like* as *lik*. *Because* looks just like it sounds except, of course, *because* is one word, not two. As she invents spelling, Kelly explores and extends her phonemic awareness of sounds and her understanding of phonics. Kelly's teacher uses Activities 1.5 (Sound Boxes with Pushing and Writing Letters) with letters in the boxes, Activity 1.8 (Stretching and Pulling Sounds), and Activity 1.14 (Spelling for Sounds) to connect sounds with letters. Activity 1.4 (Engine–Car–Caboose) normally focuses only on segmenting. However, Kelly's teacher adds letters to this activity in order to strengthen Kelly's understanding of the connection between phonemic awareness and phonics. Her teacher also uses Activity 1.13 (Blending Slide), Activity 1.15 (Grab Bag Blending), Activity 1.16 (What Am I?), and Activity 1.17 (Arm and Finger Blending) to further develop Kelly's ability to blend sounds into words.

The goal in first grade is to make sure that children have enough skill at segmenting and blending to support decoding and spelling. By the middle or end of first grade, phonics instruction, practice using phonics to sound out new words, and practice spelling new words is usually sufficient for children like Kelly to develop greater phonemic awareness. Phonemic awareness is not taught in the second grade, unless the child is struggling to use phonics as a tool for identifying and learning new words.

# REFERENCES

Birch, B. M. (2002). *English L2 reading*. Mahwah, NJ: Lawrence Erlbaum Associates.

Cassady, J. C., & Smith, L. L. (2004). Acquisition of blending skills: Comparisons among body-coda, onset-rime, and phoneme blending tasks. *Reading Psychology, 25*, 261–272.

Chiappe, P., Siegel, L. S., & Wade-Woolley, L. (2002). Linguistic diversity and the development of reading skills: A longitudinal study. *Scientific Studies of Reading, 6*, 369–400.

Christensen, C. A., & Bowey, J. A. (2005). The efficacy of orthographic rime, grapheme-phoneme correspondence, and implicit phonics approaches to teaching decoding skills. *Scientific Studies of Reading, 9*, 327–349.

Ehri, L. C., Nunes, S. R., Willows, D. M., Schuster, B. V., Yaghoub-Zadeh, Z., & Shanahan, T. (2001). Phonemic awareness instruction helps children learn to read: Evidence from the National Reading Panel's meta-analysis. *Reading Research Quarterly, 36*, 250–287.

Ehri, L. C., & Robbins, C. (1992). Beginners need some decoding skill to read words by analogy. *Reading Research Quarterly, 27*, 16–26.

Eldredge, J. L. (2005). Foundations of fluency: An exploration. *Reading Psychology, 26*, 161–181.

Geudens, A., Dominiek, S., & Van den Broeck, W. (2004). Segmenting two-phoneme syllables: Developmental differences in relation with early reading skills. *Brain and Language, 90*, 338–352.

Hatcher, P. J., Hulme, C., & Snowling, M. J. (2004). Explicit phoneme training combined with phonic reading instruction helps children at risk of reading failure. *Journal of Child Psychology and Psychiatry and Allied Disciplines, 45*, 338–350.

Hindson, B., Byrne, B., Fielding-Barnsley, R., Newman, C., Hine, D. W., & Shankweiler, D. (2005). Assessment and early instruction of preschool children at risk for reading disability. *Journal of Educational Psychology, 97*, 687–704.

Joseph, L. M. (2002). Helping children link sound to print: Phonics procedures for small-group or whole-group settings. *Intervention in School and Clinic, 37*, 217–221.

Lefstedt, J. M., & Gerber, M. M. (2005). Crossover of phonological processing skills: A study of Spanish-speaking students in two instructional settings. *Remedial and Special Education, 26*, 226–235.

Lewkowicz, N. K. (1994). The bag game: An activity to heighten phonemic awareness. *The Reading Teacher, 47*, 506–507.

Macmillan, B. M. (2002). Rhyme and reading: A critical review of the research methodology. *Journal of Research in Reading, 25*, 4–42.

Manis, F., Lindsey, K., & Bailey, C. (2004). Development of reading in grades K–2 in Spanish-speaking English-language learners. *Learning Disabilities Research & Practice, 19*, 214–224.

National Reading Panel (2000). *Teaching children to read: An evidence-based assessment of the scientific research literature on reading and its implications for reading instruction: Reports of the subgroups* (NIH Publication No. 00-4754). Washington, DC: U.S. Government Printing Office.

Quiroga, T., Lemos-Britton, Z., Mostafapour, E., Abbott, R. D., & Berninger, V. W. (2002). Phonological awareness and beginning reading in Spanish-speaking ESL first graders: Research into practice. *Journal of School Psychology, 40*, 85–111.

Schatschneider, C., Fletcher, J. M., Francis, D. J., Carlson, C. D., & Foorman, B. R. (2004). Kindergarten prediction of reading skills: A longitudinal comparative analysis. *Journal of Educational Psychology, 96*(2), 265–282.

Strattman, K., & Hodson, B. W. (2005). Variables that influence decoding and spelling in beginning readers. *Child Language Teaching and Therapy, 21*, 165–190.

Torgesen, J. K. (2002). The prevention of reading difficulties. *Journal of School Psychology, 40*, 7–26.

Yeh, S. S. (2003). An evaluation of two approaches for teaching phonemic awareness to children in Head Start. *Early Childhood Research Quarterly, 18*, 513–529.

# 2
# PHONICS

As Shandra reads aloud, she meets a word she has never seen before. The way Shandra pronounces this new word is written above the line.

> *sa  sam  same*
> Jolie and Jan are best friends. They play the *same* games.

> *sa  same*          *sss  same*
> They like the *same* things and eat the *same* food.

> *same*
> They even wear the *same* shoes.

Shandra first tries "*sa. . . sam*" and then self-corrects to read "*same*." On the second attempt, she begins with "*sa*" (the short *a* sound as in *apple*) but quickly changes to "*same*." On the third try, she says "*sss*" to herself and then reads the whole word, "*same*." The fourth time she reads *same* without sounding it out. Shandra knows a lot about phonics, about meaning, and about English sentence structure. She uses this information to sound out words. Children like Shandra who know and use phonics are better readers and better spellers in the early grades compared with children who struggle with phonics (Christensen & Bowey, 2005; National Reading Panel, 2000; Schwanenflugel, Hamilton, Kuhn, Wisenbaker, & Stahl, 2004).

## PHONICS CONTRIBUTE TO VOCABULARY AND FLUENCY

Phonics is the relationship among letters and sounds, the approach for teaching these relationships, and a shortcut for word learning. Although kindergartners and first and second graders know many spoken words, they know relatively few written words. The challenge for these children is to develop a large reading vocabulary in a short period of time. Children use phonics as a bridge between the spoken words they already know and the written words they do not recognize.

---

**BEST PRACTICES FOR EFFECTIVE TEACHING**

1. *Teach phonics early, systematically, and directly.* Children who learn phonics early and well are better readers than children who do not master phonics early (Christensen & Bowey, 2005; National Reading Panel, 2000; Schwanenflugel, Hamilton, Kuhn, Wisenbaker, & Stahl, 2004).

2. *Teach phonics along with phonemic awareness, when needed.* Teach phonics along with phonemic awareness when children are not accomplished at segmenting and blending.

3. *Follow a sequence that teaches all the important letter–sound patterns.* Following a sequence ensures that children learn the letter–sound patterns necessary for reading and spelling new words.

4. *Keep phonics meaning based.* Teach phonics directly but also teach it in conjunction with reading and writing.

5. *Teach the same letter patterns in phonics as you teach in spelling.* Teaching the same letter patterns in phonics and spelling ensures that instruction in reading and spelling support and reinforce each other (Ehri, 2000).

---

Phonics makes it possible for children to learn new words. When children use phonics they pay careful attention to the letters in words. Paying attention to the letters in words helps children remember words the next time they see them. The more children analyze, read, and write the same words, the stronger the memory, and the faster the recognition (Ehri, 2004). Eventually, the sounds, spellings, and meanings of words are bundled together in memory. Children then recognize these words instantly, at a glance. Automatic or instant word recognition occurs without conscious effort.

Phonics does not cause fluency, but it does contribute to fluency through its effect on vocabulary (Eldredge, 2005). Phonics helps children learn to instantly recognize words. Instant word recognition, in turn, makes it possible for children to read expressively, accurately, and at a pace appropriate for the text and the reading situation. Instant word recognition also makes it possible for children to concentrate on meaning because children do not have to worry about figuring out the words. Not surprisingly, children who are good at phonics are more fluent readers and better comprehenders, regardless of children's social or economic background (Christensen & Bowey, 2005; National Reading Panel, 2000; Schwanenflugel, Hamilton, Kuhn, Wisenbaker, & Stahl, 2004).

## LETTER–SOUND PATTERNS

The 26 single letters are divided into two groups of five vowels and twenty-one consonants. The vowels letters are *a, e, i, o, u,* with *y* and *w* occasionally acting as vowels. The remaining letters are consonants. Consonants are relatively predictable in the way they represent sounds. We might think of consonants as the backbone of words. For instance, we can read Th_se _r_ c_ns_n_nt l_tt_rs even though the vowels are missing. If the consonants are the backbone of words, the vowels are the heart. English words have at least one vowel. In fact, a couple of words consist of only vowels—*I, a.* The vowels are not as consistent as the consonants. For one thing, vowel letters represent more than one sound (*made, mad*). For another thing, sometimes the same vowel sound is spelled in a variety of ways (*how, house*). Table 2–1 shows the consonant letter–sounds and examples of words that include these letter–sounds. Table 2–2 shows the different ways we combine vowels to represent various sounds and words that illustrate these spellings.

---

**TABLE 2–1  Consonant Patterns for Word Study**

---

### Double Consonants

Double consonants occur in the middle (*rabbit*) or at the end (*miss*) of a word. One consonant sound is heard; the other is silent.

| | |
|---|---|
| *bb* | *rabbit, ebb, ribbon* |
| *dd* | *hidden, ladder, puddle* |
| *ff* | *waffle, coffee, muffin* |
| *ll* | *jelly, bell, pillow* |
| *mm* | *summer, hammer, command* |
| *nn* | *dinner, minnow, funnel* |
| *pp* | *puppet, copper, happen* |
| *rr* | *carrot, burro, narrow* |
| *zz* | *buzz, drizzle, pizza* |

### Consonant Blends

Consonant blends consist of two or three consonants that are blended together when pronounced (*down, spray*). (Some teachers' manuals use the term clusters to refer to the consonant blends.) Consonant blends are taught as whole-letter patterns rather than as single letters (e.g., *st* as representing two blended phonemes /st/, rather than an isolated /s/ and an isolated /t/). The most common blends occur at the beginning of words or syllables and include the letters *r, l* and *s*.

| Blends | Words | *l* Blends | Words | *s* Blends | Words | *w* Blends | Words |
|---|---|---|---|---|---|---|---|
| *br* | *bright* | *bl* | *black* | *sc* | *scout* | *dw* | *dwell* |
| *cr* | *crayon* | *cl* | *class* | *scr* | *scream* | *sw* | *swing* |
| *dr* | *dress* | *fl* | *flower* | *sk* | *sky* | *tw* | *twin* |
| *fr* | *free* | *gl* | *glad* | *sm* | *small* | | |
| *gr* | *green* | *pl* | *plan* | *sn* | *snow* | | |
| *pr* | *pretty* | *sl* | *slide* | *sp* | *spot* | | |
| *shr* | *shrink* | | | *spl* | *splash* | | |
| *thr* | *three* | | | *spr* | *spring* | | |
| *tr* | *train* | | | *squ* | *square* | | |
| | | | | *st* | *stop* | | |
| | | | | *str* | *string* | | |

Some consonant blends occur at the end of English words or syllables. Final blends are sometimes taught as part of word families, such as *old* (*told*), *ild* (*wild*), *ilk* (*milk*), and *alt* (*salt*).

| Final Blends | Words | Final Blends | Words |
|---|---|---|---|
| *ct* | *fact* | *nch* | *bunch* |
| *ft* | *lift* | *nd* | *end* |
| *ld* | *old* | *nk* | *pink* |
| *lk* | *milk* | *nt* | *went* |
| *lp* | *help* | *pt* | *kept* |
| *lt* | *salt* | *sk* | *desk* |
| *mp* | *jump* | *sp* | *grasp* |
| | | *st* | *last* |

The *l* in *lk* is frequently silent: *balk, chalk, folk, stalk, talk, walk, yolk*. If you hear /l/ in these words, it is because of regional dialect.

**TABLE 2–1** (*Continued*)

## Consonant Digraphs

Consonant digraphs consist of two letters that represent one sound, and that sound is different from the sound that the letters individually represent.

| Digraphs | Words | Digraphs | Words |
|---|---|---|---|
| ch | chair | ck | thick* |
| ph | phone | dg | fudge |
| sh | shoe | ng | king |
| unvoiced th | thumb | nk | think |
| voiced th | that | | |
| wh | whale | | |

We pronounce *th* two different ways: The unvoiced *th* is whispered, as in *think*. We use our vocal cords to pronounce the voiced *th*, as in *this*.

*\*ck* represents /k/ at the end of words or syllables with a short vowel.

## c + Vowel Pattern

The letter *c* represents two sounds: (1) a hard sound as heard in *cat*, and (2) a soft sound as in *city*. The *c* usually represents /k/ (the hard sound) when followed by a (*cat*), o (*coat*), or u (*cut*), when it appears at the end of a word (*comic*), and when followed by any other letter (*cloud*). *C* usually represents /s/ (the soft sound) when it is followed by e (*cent*), i (*city*), or y (*cycle*).

| c plus a, o, u | Words | c plus e, i, y, | Words |
|---|---|---|---|
| ca | cat (/k/) (hard sound) | ce (/s/) | cent (soft sound) |
| co | coat (k) (hard sound) | ci (/s/) | city (soft sound) |
| cu | cut (/k/) (hard sound) | cy (/s/) | cycle (soft sound) |

## g + Vowel Pattern

The letter *g* represents two sounds: (1) a hard sound, as heard in *goat*, and (2) a soft sound, as heard in *gem*. *G* usually represents /g/ (the hard sound) when it is followed by a (*gate*), o (*go*), or u (*gum*), when it appears at the end of a word (*leg*), and when followed by any other consonant letter (*glass*). *G* may represent /j/ (the soft sound) when it is followed by the vowels e (*gerbil*), i (*giant*), or y (*gypsy*), although with more exceptions than ga, go, and gu.

| g plus a, o, u | Words | g plus e, i, y | Words |
|---|---|---|---|
| ga | gate (hard sound) | ge | gerbil (soft sound) |
| go | go (hard sound) | gi | giant (soft sound) |
| gu | gum (hard sound) | gy | gypsy (soft sound) |

## Silent Letters

Some letters are silent; that is, they do not represent a sound. There are eight silent letter patterns: *mb, bt, ght, gn, kn, lk, tch,* and *wr.*

| Silent Pattern | Words | Explanation |
|---|---|---|
| bt | doubt | *B* is silent when preceding *t* in a syllable. |
| ght | night | *Gh* is silent when preceding *t* in a syllable. |
| gn | align | *G* is silent following *n* in a syllable. |
| kn | knight | *K* is silent when preceding *n* at the beginning of words. |
| lk | chalk | *L* is silent when preceding *k* in a syllable. |
| mb | bomb | *B* is silent following *m* in a syllable. |
| tch | witch | *T* is silent when preceding *ch* in a syllable. |
| wr | write | *W* is silent when preceding *r* at the beginning of words. |

---

**TABLE 2–2  Vowel Patterns for Word Study**

---

| Short Vowels | Symbols | Key Words | Long Vowels | Symbols | Key words |
|---|---|---|---|---|---|
| a | ă | apple | a | ā | apron |
| e | ĕ | egg | e | ē | eraser |
| i | ĭ | igloo | i | ī | ice |
| o | ŏ | ox | o | ō | overalls |
| u | ŭ | umbrella | u | ū | unicorn |

We use ă to indicate short vowels sounds, and ā to indicate long vowel sounds.

### VC Short Vowel Pattern

The most common vowel–consonant pattern is that of the VC (vowel–consonant) in which the V (vowel) represents its short sound. One, two, or three consonants may precede the vowel in the VC pattern.

| Vowel | Words with a VC Pattern |
|---|---|
| a + Consonant | at, man, pat, trap |
| e + Consonant | etch, bed, pet, step |
| i + Consonant | it, hit, spin, trip |
| o + Consonant | ox, nod, pot, top |
| u + Consonant | up, bus, drum, shut |

### VCCe Short Vowel Pattern

When the V (vowel) is followed by two consonants and a final e (VCCe), we usually use a short sound when pronouncing the first vowel and the final e is silent.

| VCCe Pattern | Words |
|---|---|
| aCCe | badge, dance, lapse |
| eCCe | edge, fence, sense |
| iCCe | bridge, rinse, since |
| uCCe | fudge, plunge |

### VCe Long Vowel Pattern

When a V (vowel) is followed by a consonant and a final e (VCe), the e is silent and the first vowel usually represents the long sound.

| VCe Pattern | Words |
|---|---|
| aCe | ate, cake, made, name |
| iCe | ice, dime, like, smile |
| oCe | cone, home, joke, rope |
| uCe | use, cute, huge, mule |

### CV Long Vowel Pattern

The vowel is usually long in words and syllables that end in a vowel letter and vowel sound (CV).

| CV Pattern | Words |
|---|---|
| Consonant + ay | day, may, play |
| Consonant + e | be, he, me |
| Consonant + o | go, no, so |
| Consonant + y | by, my, try |

---

**TABLE 2–2 (*Continued*)**

---

### VV Long Vowel Pattern

In the V V pattern, two vowels appear together in a word or syllable. The first vowel usually represents the long sound and the second vowel is silent. Some vowel pairs follow the generalization more consistently than others. This pattern is also called vowel pairs or vowel teams.

| VV | Words |
|----|-------|
| *ai* | *mail, paid, rain, train* |
| *ay* | *day, may, say, way* |
| *oa* | *boat, goal, road, soak* |
| *ea* | *each, heat, leaf, mean* |
| *ee* | *feet, keep, meet, sleep* |
| *ie* | *die, lie, pie, tie* |

### Diphthongs

A diphthong is a single-vowel phoneme, represented by two letters, which resembles a glide from one sound to another. We teach children about two diphthong sounds. Two different letter combinations represent each sound. (1) Both *ou* and *ow* represent the same sound. When this sound is heard at the beginning (ouch) and middle (couch) of a word, it is represented by the letters *ou*; when this sound appears at the end of a word (cow) or syllable (power), the sound is represented by the letters *ow*. (2) Both *oi* and *oy* represent the same sound. When this sound is heard at the beginning (oink) or in the middle (coin) of a word, it is represented by the letters *oi*. When this sound is heard at the end of a word (boy) or syllable (foyer), it is represented by the letters *oy*.

| Diphthong Pairs | Words | Diphthong Pairs | Words |
|----|-------|----|-------|
| *ou* | *cloud, count, mouse* | *oi* | *boil, coin, soil* |
| *ow* | *brown, fowl, town* | *oy* | *boy, joy, toy* |

### Oo v Pattern

| oo Pattern | Words |
|----|-------|
| *oo* | *f<u>oo</u>d, broom, moon, school* |
| *oo* | *h<u>oo</u>k, book, good, look* |

### Vr (r-controlled) Pattern

When the only vowel letter in a word or syllable is followed by *r*, the vowel will be affected by that *r*, and the vowel sound is almost lost in the consonant.

| Vr | Words |
|----|-------|
| *ar* | *car, hard, jar* |
| *er* | *after, her, over* |
| *ir* | *bird, circle, shirt* |
| *or* | *corn, more, store* |
| *ur* | *fur, hurt, turn* |

**TABLE 2.2  (Continued)**

**a Followed by l, ll, w, and u**

The letter *a* often represents the sound in *salt* (al), *tall* (all), *saw* (aw), and *haul* (au) when followed by *l, ll, w,* and *u*.

| *al* | Words | *all* | Words | *aw* | Words | *au* | Words |
|------|-------|-------|-------|------|-------|------|-------|
| al | almost | all | call | aw | draw | au | because |
|    | bald  |     | fall  |    | law   |    | fault   |
|    | halt  |     | tall  |    | saw   |    | haul    |

**Vowels in Unaccented Syllables**

The vowel in an unaccented syllable usually represents a soft "uh," or the sound we associate with short *i*. The dictionary uses a schwa(ə) to indicate the soft "uh" sound in many unaccented syllables. The vowel in unaccented syllables represents the soft "uh" more often than the short *i*.

| Schwa("uh") | Examples |
|-------------|----------|
| a(ə) | comm*a* (soft "uh") |
| e(ə) | chick*en* (soft "uh") |
| i (ə) | fam*ily* (soft "uh") |
| o(ə) | butt*on* (soft "uh") |
| u(ə) | circ*us* (soft "uh") |

Beginning readers use the letter–sound patterns of phonics to decode. For example, they sound out *boat* by associating a sound with each pattern (*b* = /b/, *oa* = /oa/, *t* = /t/) and blend the sounds into a word (/b/ + /oa/ + /t/ = /boat/). Beginning readers also use rimes to figure out the sounds of new words. A rime is the vowel and the consonants that follow it in a syllable. The *ad* in *sad* and the *all* in *stall* are rimes. An onset is the beginning letter–sound (the *s* in *sad* and the *st* in *stall*). Word families are groups of words that share the same rime (*lamp, stamp, cramp*). The vowels in rimes are consistent, which makes rimes relatively easy to read. Decoding and spelling word-family words can be a stepping-stone to word learning. However, there are too many vowel–consonant combinations in English to make it feasible for children to use only rimes to decode. The children whom you teach will make faster progress learning to read when they decode by associating sounds with letters rather than associating sounds *only* with onsets and rimes (Johnston & Watson, 2004). (See pages 48–61, "Informal Assessment or Additional Practices for Observing and Developing Good Decoders.")

# ACTIVITIES

## 17 ACTIVITIES TO DEVELOP DECODING

### 2.1   Fan Books

- Small group
- Use to develop knowledge of word-family rimes or letter–sound patterns.

Fan books have graduated pages so that readers immediately see the word family or letter-sound on each page.

**Material:** Six sheets of unlined 8½-×-11 construction paper per child; markers or pencils; rulers; stapler.

**Step-by-step directions:**

1. Measure 1 inch from the 8½-inch side of one sheet of paper. Draw a vertical line along the 8½-inch edge. Cut the 1-inch strip off. This leaves a page 10 inches long.

2. Pick up a second sheet. Use your ruler to measure 2 inches from the 8½-inch edge. Draw a vertical line and cut off 2 inches. The second paper is now 9 inches long.

3. Cut 3 inches from the end of the third sheet (now 8 inches long). Cut 4 inches from the fourth sheet (now 7 inches long). Cut 6 inches from the sixth sheet (now 5 inches long).

4. Put your book together. Put the 10-inch sheet flat on a table. Put the 9-inch sheet on top of the 10-inch sheet, followed by the 8-inch sheet, and so on. Continue stacking paper until the shortest page is on the top.

5. Staple the edge of the fan book.

6. Children write a word family or phonics pattern on each page. Figure 2–1 shows a word-family fan book made by a first grader.

**Figure 2–1**
Word-Family Fan Book

*Continued on p. 34*

**Figure 2–1**
*Continued*

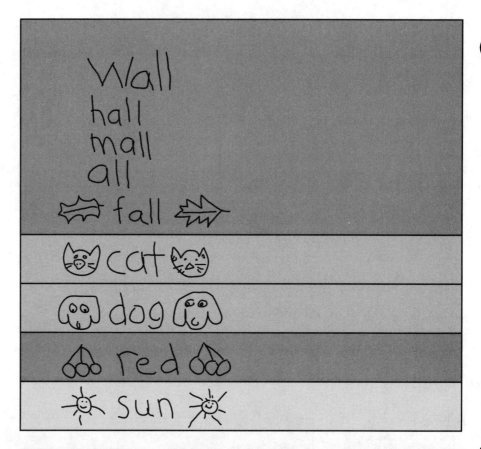

**Figure 2–1**
*Continued*

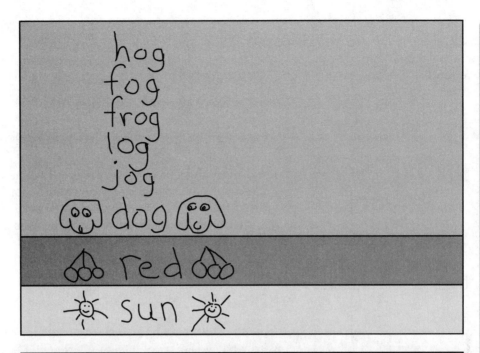

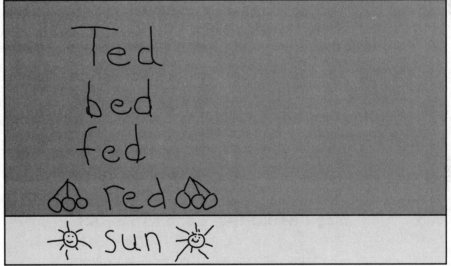

## 2.2   Vowel Hopscotch

**Figure 2–2**
Vowel Hopscotch

*Hopscotch gives children practice pronouncing words spelled with contrasting vowel patterns.*

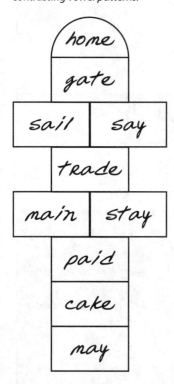

- Small group or pairs
- Use to develop knowledge of vowel patterns.

This paper-and-pencil adaptation of hopscotch gives children practice identifying long- and short-vowel words.

**Material:** Hopscotch patterns with words in squares that are spelled with the vowel patterns children are learning; tokens; hopscotch patterns on overhead transparencies. Make transparencies with different hopscotch patterns and words. You also will need as many hopscotch patterns on paper as there are pairs of players. Write words in the squares that are spelled with the vowel patterns children are learning, as shown in Figure 2–2.

**Step-by-step directions:**

1. Show the children a hopscotch transparency. Have children read each word while you or a volunteer underline it. Use red for long-vowel patterns, blue for short to call attention to vowels. (Figure 2–2.)

2. Once children have enough competence to play vowel hopscotch with a partner, give each pair a piece of paper with a different hopscotch pattern or place hopscotch papers in a learning center.

3. Two children take turns reading words in hopscotch squares and moving a token into a square for each word read. Children may take turns hopping on the squares one after the other from start to finish.

## 2.3   Magic *e* Fold-Overs and Flip Books

- Small group, pairs, individual, or learning center
- Use to develop knowledge of the VCe (*can–cane*) long-vowel pattern.

Children learn how the addition of a silent *e* turns a VC (*can*) short-vowel word into a VCe (*cane*) long-vowel word. Use fold-overs and flip books with children who struggle with reading VCe words, as shown in Figure 2–3.

**Material:** Sentence strips; felt pen; two metal rings; strips of poster board.

**Step-by-step directions:**

**Fold-Overs**

1. Cut sentence strips into 6-inch sections. Fold the end back. Write a VC word on the longer section and an *e* on the section you have folded back.

2. Demonstrate how a VC short-vowel word changes into a VCe long-vowel word by (1) folding the silent *e* behind the VC word and (2) straightening the card to reveal the *e*, VCe word.

3. Have children make their own silent *e* fold-overs. Place fold-overs in learning centers or ask pairs to take turns reading the silent *e* fold-overs.

### Flip Books

1. Cut strips of poster board about 6 inches long and one strip about 8 inches long. Write short-vowel words on the short strips and a final *e* on the far right of the long strip. Punch two holes in the cards (Figure 2–4).

2. Children flip through the pages reading each word as it appears.

3. Ask pairs to read the books to each other or have a small group read the words in chorus. Table 2–3 has many short-vowel words that become long-vowel words when a final *e* is added.

**Figure 2–3**
Magic *e* Fold-Overs

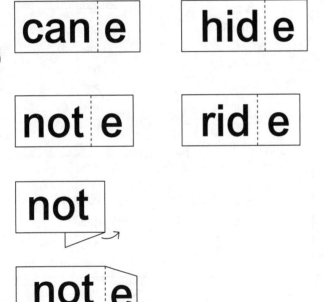

**Figure 2–4**
Magic *e* Flip Book

*As children turn pages of the flip book they develop insight into how adding a final e changes short-vowel words into long-vowel words.*

**TABLE 2–3  Short-Vowel Words That Make Long-Vowel Silent *e* Words**

| Short-Vowel Words | Long-Vowel Final *e* Words | Short-Vowel Words | Long-Vowel Final *e* Words |
|---|---|---|---|
| bit | bite | pan | pane |
| can | cane | pet | Pete |
| cap | cape | pin | pine |
| cod | code | plan | plane |
| con | cone | prim | prime |
| cop | cope | rat | rate |
| cub | cube | rid | ride |
| cut | cute | rip | ripe |
| dim | dime | rob | robe |
| dot | dote | rod | rode |
| dud | dude | Sam | same |
| fad | fade | shin | shine |
| fat | fate | slid | slide |
| fin | fine | slim | slime |
| gap | gape | slop | slope |
| glad | glade | snip | snipe |
| glob | globe | spin | spine |
| grim | grime | tap | tape |
| grip | gripe | Tim | time |
| hid | hide | tot | tote |
| hop | hope | twin | twine |
| hug | huge | scrap | scrape |
| kit | kite | snip | snipe |
| lob | lobe | spit | spite |
| lop | lope | strip | stripe |
| mad | made | trip | tripe |
| man | mane | tub | tube |
| mat | mate | twin | twine |
| mop | mope | wad | wade |
| rod | rode | wag | wage |
| not | note | | |

## 2.4    Scooping

- Small group, pairs, individual, or learning center
- Use to develop knowledge of letter–sound patterns.

Children divide words into letter–sound patterns by drawing "scoops" (half circles) under patterns.

**Material:** For scooping you will need text children can write on and words from familiar books that are spelled with the letter patterns children are learning.

**Step-by-step directions:**

1. Ask children to scoop (draw half circles under) letter–sound patterns as they sound out words. For example, children would put two scoops under *stray* and three under *church*.

s t r a y          c h u r c h

2. Focus on one or two patterns at a time. For instance, you might focus on scooping short-vowel (VC) (*cap*) and final *e* long-vowel words (VCe) (*cape*). Or you might focus only on the single pattern, as the r-controlled pattern in *car* and *first*.

s l i d        s l i d e        h o p        h o p e

m a d        m a d e

## 2.5   Picking What Works for Me

- Pairs, individual or learning center
- Use to develop strategy use while reading.

This activity gives children practice selecting word identification strategies.

**Material:** One small flower pot per child; popsicles with "flowers" glued to them. Write phonics strategies on the flowers. Put flowers in the pot. You might want to put clay in the bottom of the pot for stability (Figure 2–5).

**Figure 2–5**
Picking What Works for Me

*Popsicle stick flowers prompt readers to use the word identity strategies you are teaching.*

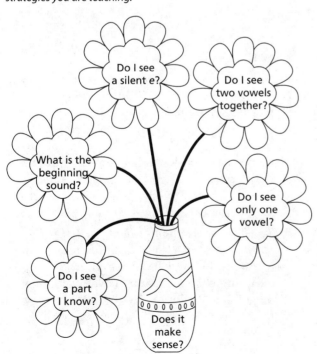

**Step-by-step directions:**

1. Write "Does It Make Sense?" on the side of the pot and place strategy flowers inside the pot.

2. Give each child a flower pot with strategy choices.

3. Children choose and use a strategy to decode a new word.

4. Change strategies as appropriate for children's needs.

   Suggestions for strategies:

   A. Do I see a part I know?

   B. What is the beginning sound?

   C. Do I see a silent *e*?

   D. Do I see two vowels together?

   E. Do I see only one vowel?

5. Follow up by asking children, "What strategy did you pick? Why?" "Did anyone pick something different?" "What other choices might we add to the flower pot?" "Does the word make sense?"

## 2.6    Tents

- Small group, pairs, or individual
- Use to develop knowledge of letter–sound patterns and to give children practice reading words spelled with these patterns.

Children use their fingers to "jump over" paper tents that have words spelled with the letter–sound patterns they are learning (Figure 2–6).

**Material:** Unlined 3 × 5 cards; black marker. Write words with the letter-sound patterns children are learning on cards. Fold the cards in half and place them in a line around the edge of the table, as shown in Figure 2–6.

**Step-by-step directions:**

1. Place the tents along the edge of a table. The child "jumps" the tents by touching the table beside each word while saying the words on the tent. Have the child read the word tents several times.
2. The child must read each word correctly before going on to the next.
3. Just for fun you may wish to time how fast each child jumps the tents and then challenge children to beat their own time.
4. Rearrange the tents after each set of jumps.

**Figure 2–6**
Tents

### TEACHING ENGLISH LANGUAGE LEARNERS

1. *Supplement phonics instruction, when necessary.* Supplemental phonics instruction improves the decoding skills, vocabulary, comprehension, and fluency of English learners who read below grade level (Gunn, Smolkowski, Biglan, & Black, 2002; Lesaux & Siegel, 2003; Otaiba, 2005).

2. *Teach phonics over a sustained period of time.* Because many English learners tend to learn phonics at a slower rate, instruction needs to be provided over a longer period of time than is typical for the average English-speaking child (Denton, Anthony, Parker, & Hasbrouck, 2004; Gunn, Smolkowski, Biglan, & Black, 2002).

3. *Integrate phonics with comprehension.* While teaching phonics results in better decoding, it does not necessarily result in better language comprehension (Stuart, 2004), unless it is integrated with comprehension and discussions of meaning (Araujo, 2002).

4. *Ask children to sound out words they understand.* When children sound out words they do not understand they merely change an unfamiliar printed word into an unfamiliar spoken word. This does not further comprehension or help English learners develop a large English reading vocabulary. Look in chapter 5 for suggestions on teaching word meaning.

5. *Teach the same phonics sequence to English learners and English-only children.* English learners and English-only children develop decoding skills in a similar way (Chiappe, Siegel, & Wade-Woolley, 2002; Rupley, Rodriquez, Mergen, Willson, & Nichols, 2000).

## 2.7    Caterpillar

- Small group
- Use to develop knowledge of letter–sound patterns.

A small group makes caterpillars that consist of words spelled with the letter–sound patterns they are learning.

**Material:** Words on construction paper circles; two construction paper circles with eyes, nose, mouth, and tentacles for caterpillar heads; tape or thumbtacks.

**Step-by-step directions:**

1. Fasten two caterpillar "heads" to a bulletin board. Explain that the first caterpillar consists of words spelled with one pattern—for example, *oa*—the other with a different pattern, perhaps *ee* (see Tables 2–1 and 2–2 for explanations and ideas).
2. Give each child in a small group a handful of colorful round cards with words that are spelled with the patterns.
3. Children read the words and decide which caterpillar the words belong (Figure 2–7).
4. Ask children to read each caterpillar in chorus.
5. Change the caterpillars as children learn new phonics patterns.

**Figure 2–7**
Word Caterpillar

*Children add words spelled with the same letter–sound patterns to make word caterpillars.*

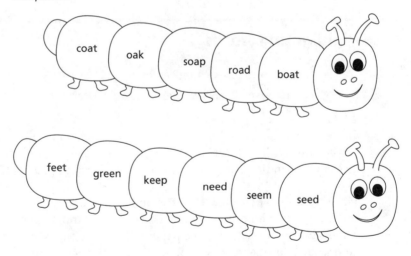

## 2.8    Chains

- Small group, pairs, or learning center
- Use to develop knowledge of letter–sound patterns.

Children make chains for words spelled with the same letter–sound patterns.

**Figure 2–8**
Chain

*Making construction paper chains calls for thinking about, writing, and reading words spelled with the letter–sound patterns children are learning.*

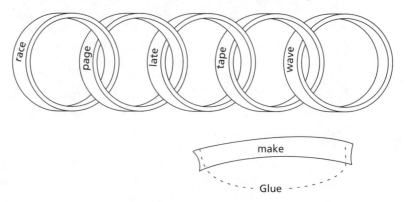

**Material:** Construction paper strips with words; glue stick or stapler.

**Step-by-step directions:**

1. Cut colorful construction paper into strips. Write words with several letter–sound patterns on the strips. Put all the strips in a large envelope.
2. Three children take the words out of the envelope and place them face down on a table. Taking turns, each child turns over a strip and reads the word. Words that do not fit the pattern go back in the envelope. Words that fit the pattern are added to the chain by gluing (or stapling) the ends of the strip together, as shown in Figure 2–8.

## 2.9   Highlighting Words

- Small group or learning center
- Use to develop knowledge of vowel patterns.

This is a good center activity for children who need just a bit more practice identifying vowel patterns. If children are struggling with these patterns, you will want to improve their understanding using steps 1 and 2 below before placing the activity in centers.

**Material:** Copies of sentences with familiar words; two different color highlighters, perhaps red and blue; copies of text on overhead transparencies for the purpose of demonstrating the activity; one paper with sentences for each child or pair in a small group. Try to use sentences from the books children are reading to forge a strong connection between this activity and the words children read in the text in your classroom.

**Step-by-step directions:**

1. Ask everyone in a small group to read the text on an overhead in chorus. Demonstrate how to highlight short vowels in blue, long vowels in red.
2. Then ask children to identify some of the short- and long-vowel words on the overhead. Use red or blue to highlight these words.

3. Give children their own copies of sentences you have prepared. Ask children to work in pairs or individually to highlight the long- and short-vowel words.

4. Monitor children's work. Create a small skills group for children who find this activity difficult; model how to identify different patterns; provide teacher guided practice until children are able to try highlighting on their own.

## 2.10    Trading Letters

- Small group
- Use to develop knowledge of vowel patterns.

Children trade letters to spell words with different vowel patterns. This is an effective way to improve decoding, especially for children who do not pay close attention to all the letter–sound patterns in words (McCandliss, Beck, Sandak, & Perfetti, 2003).

**Material:** Letter cards.

**Step-by-step directions:**

1. Give children in a small group several letter cards.
2. Ask children to spell a word, such as *mad*, and have them change just one letter to make another word, such as *made*.
3. Talk about the patterns; ask children to explain the sounds that the patterns represent.

| change | f | i | n | to | f | i | n | e | (VC to VCe pattern) |

| change | c | a | t | to | c | a | r | t | (VC to r-controlled pattern) |

| change | b | e | t | to | b | e | e | t | (VC to VV pattern) |

## 2.11    Rime Roads

- Small group
- Use to develop knowledge of word-family rimes.

Children pair onsets (beginning consonants) with rimes to make words.

**Material:** Consonant and rime patterns on cards.

**Step-by-step directions:**

1. Sketch three or four roads on the board, as we see in Figure 2–9.
2. Put onsets (beginning consonants) cards in the chalk tray.

**Figure 2–9**
Rime Roads

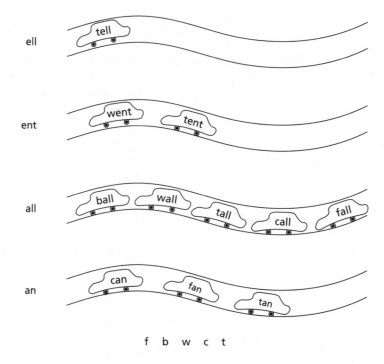

3.  Children make "cars" by combining onsets with rimes.

4.  Write the words (cars) on each road or ask volunteers to write the words.

5.  Review the words (cars) when the children have made as many words (cars) as possible with the onset-rime combinations. Have individuals read all the words on one road. For additional practice, have the group read the words in chorus; point to each word as it is read.

## 2.12    Duck, Duck, Goose

- Small group
- Use to develop knowledge of word-family rimes.

This adaptation of the game Duck, Duck, Goose gives children practice reading word-family words.

**Material:** Cards with word-family words.

**Step-by-step directions:**

1.  Children sit in chairs around a table or in a circle on the floor. If children sit around a table have them turn their chairs around so the backs of the chairs touch the table and the children sit facing away from the table.

2.  One child is "It." It has a card with a word-family word. It keeps the card hidden.

3.  It walks slowly around the circle. (It gently taps each child on the head in the original version of Duck, Duck, Goose.) If It makes too many trips around the

circle, tell the children that It can go around the circle once. On the second trip It must tap a child.

4. Without warning, It stops in front of a child and shows the child the word. The child reads the word.

5. If successful the child become the new It. Give the new It another word-family card.

## 2.13   Race and Chase

**Figure 2–10**
Race and Chase

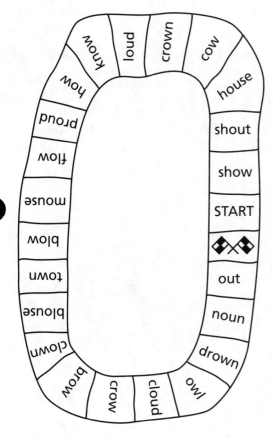

- Pairs or learning center
- Use to develop knowledge of letter–sound patterns.

Children take turns moving around a racetrack tokens with words that are spelled with the patterns children are learning.

**Material:** Laminated piece of tag board with a racetrack that is divided into squares, a spinner, and two tokens. Write words in the squares that are spelled with patterns children are learning (Figure 2–10).

**Step-by-step directions:**

1. Two children play this game together. Place word cards face down. The first child draws a card. If the child reads the word, the child spins the spinner and moves a token as many spaces as indicated.

2. Children take turns reading words and moving around the track until one child reaches the end.

3. Suggestions for long-vowel words: *boat, go, snow, those, grow, goal, load, no, home, those, deep, me, tree, key, see, honey, heat, leaf, leap, try, kite, night, pie, ice, fly, sigh, like, mine, play, date, trade, mail, rain, came, lay, safe, bake, cube, rule, mule, cute, huge, June.*

## 2.14   Word-Family Eggs

- Pairs, individual, or learning center
- Use to develop knowledge of word-family rimes.

Children make words by putting together plastic eggs that have beginning letters and rimes on them.

**Material:** Plastic eggs split in half with beginning sounds on one half and word-family rimes on the other. Leave eggs intact. Write a beginning sound on one half and a word-family rime on the other. Separate eggs.

**Step-by-step directions:**

1.  Place the egg halves in a basket. Put the basket in a learning center or give it to individuals or pairs.
2.  Ask children to make as many words as they can by combining half an egg with a beginning letter with a half that has a word-family rime.
3.  Children read and then write the words.
4.  Eggs do not have to have the same color halves. The two combined halves have to make a word that children recognize and can read.

## 2.15    Finding Lost Dogs (or Cats)

*   Small group
*   Use to develop knowledge of word family rimes or letter–sound patterns.

Children find words you have placed in strategic places around the room that are spelled with the patterns children are learning.

**Material:** Word cards spelled with the patterns children are learning; "dog houses" that consist of construction paper with the spelling pattern written on the top (Figure 2–11).

**Figure 2–11**
Finding Lost Dogs

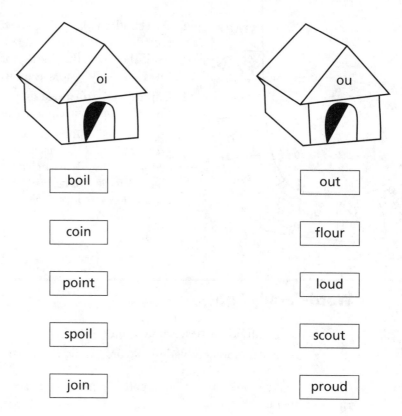

**Step-by-step directions:**

1. Place stacks of word cards strategically around the room. Assign a special "dog" to each child. Suggestions for "dogs" the children might look for include: (1) long-vowel dogs, such as VCe long *a* (*made*), *i* (*hide*), *o* (*rode*) or VV (vowel-vowel) *oa* (*boat*), *ai* (*rain*), *ee* (*tree*); (2) diphthong dogs divided into *ow* (*down*), *ou* (*house*), *oi* (*oil*), and *oy* (*toy*); (3) consonant digraph and blend dogs; (4) rime dogs (*ock* dogs, *ell* dogs, and *ing* dogs, for example).

2. Tell each child to look for "dogs" with a special pattern, as described above. Children look in the parking lot (on your desk or work space), along the road (in the chalk tray), on the playground (on the window sills), or in the library (in the area where books are kept).

3. Before the "dogs" are returned to their owner, each child reads the words and then places the "dogs" in a "house" with the proper pattern (Figure 2–11).

---

## 2.16   100-Yard Dash

**Figure 2–12**
100-Yard Dash

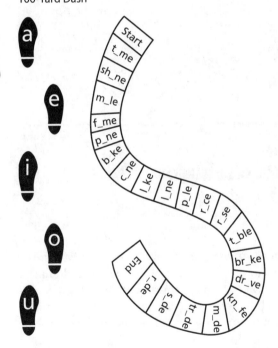

- Pairs or learning center
- Use to develop knowledge of word-family rimes or letter–sound patterns.

This board game has words inside a path with a letter replaced by a blank (see Figure 2–12). Children build words by selecting a letter on the game board to combine with the letters in each square.

**Materials:** Poster board; marker; shoe patterns with a letter (or letters) on each one. Make the game by drawing a path on the poster board. Draw lines to create sections. Write a word in each section, omitting one letter. Write words that are spelled with patterns or word-family rimes the children are learning.

**Step-by-step directions:**

1. Players put tokens on *Start*. Players take turns spinning a spinner or tossing one die to see how far to move.

2. Each player combines a word on the square with the letter on any one of the shoes to make a real word. The player then reads the word.

3. If a player cannot make a real word, the player returns to the previous square.

4. The first player who reaches *End* wins.

## 2.17    Accordion Books

**Figure 2–13**
Accordion Book for the *ar* Pattern

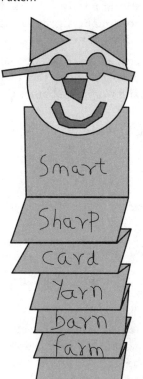

- Small group; portions of this activity can be done in a learning center
- Use to develop knowledge of word-family rimes or letter–sound patterns.

Children find words with the letter patterns or word-family rimes they are learning and make folded accordion books that feature the patterns.

**Material:** Sturdy construction paper strips, 3 inches wide; glue sticks or stapler; scissors; colored construction paper for making a face or character in the books children are reading.

**Step-by-step directions:**

1. Give children one strip of colored construction paper. Children fold the strip accordion style, leaving about 3 inches on one end.
2. Children write a letter pattern or word-family word on each fold.
3. Glue or staple a colorful face to the top of the accordion books (Figure 2–13). Children read their books, share the books with their classmates, and take books home to share with their families.

---

# INFORMAL ASSESSMENT OR ADDITIONAL PRACTICES FOR OBSERVING AND DEVELOPING GOOD DECODERS

## Additional Practices

*Show children how to connect rhyme and beginning-sound awareness with reading and spelling.* Demonstrating how to read and spell words with onsets and shared rimes brings together (1) rhyme awareness, (2) beginning-sound awareness, (3) beginning letter–sounds (phonics), and (4) rime letter–sound knowledge (phonics). Demonstrating also gives children a model to imitate, clears up any confusion in the child's mind, and speeds the learning process along. Generally speaking, spelling and reading word-family words is much easier for the beginning reader than sounding out words with phonics. You can expect to spend less time modeling the spelling and reading of word-family words than modeling spelling and writing with phonics. Have children follow your lead by using their own letter cards to spell and read word-family words. In this example, you would give each child in a small group letter and rime cards for *m*, *f*, *p*, *r*, *an*, and *un*.

1. Write *man* on the board. Ask children to put the *m* and *an* cards side-by-side from left to right. Say the sound associated with the letter *m*, /mmmm/, and the sounds associated with the *an*, /aaannn/. Point to the letters as you

pronounce the sounds. Sweep your hand under the letters as you blend the sounds.

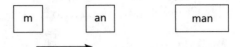

2. Replace the *m* with an *f* and have the children associate the /f/ with the letter *f* and the /an/ with the *an* card. Then demonstrate and practice blending. Sweep your hand under the letters as you pronounce the sounds, /fff-faaaannnn/. Then ask, "What's the new word?"

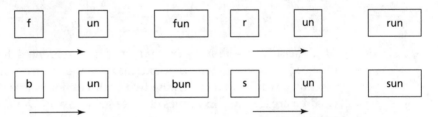

3. Replace *an* with *un*. Pronounce /fffuuunnn/ while sweeping your hand under each letter as you blend the sounds together. Have the children repeat blending /fffuuunnn/. Ask, "What's this word?" Continue making and blending other words.

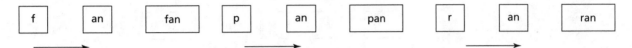

***Show children how to connect segmenting and blending with reading and spelling.*** Follow these steps to demonstrate how to combine phonemic awareness and letter–sound knowledge to read and spell new words one letter-sound pattern at a time. We will use the words *sat, sit, set,* and *pet* for the purposes of illustration.

1. Give children letter cards for *s, p, t, a, i* and *e*. Have children put the *s, a,* and *t* cards from left to right on their tables. Write the letters *s, a, t* on the board.

2. Point to each letter and pronounce the sound associated with it. Make sure that children point to each letter as you say the sound. Have the children join you in saying the sounds associated with the letters.

3. Demonstrate blending by stretching out the sounds and saying them together with the children. Sweep your hand under the two letters on the board as you pronounce "sssaaaa." Have the children imitate your voice, pointing to the letters on their tables as they blend /sssaaaa/.

4. Remind children that *t* represents /t/. Although we cannot effectively stretch the /t/ sound, we can emphasize this sound as we say it, /t/. Blend /sssaaaat/ while sweeping your hand under each letter as you blend the sounds together. Have the children repeat blending /sssaaat/. Ask, "What's this word?"

5. Erase the *a* and write *i* on the board. Ask children to take away the *a* and put an *i* in its place. Sound stretch /sssiiit/. Sweep your hand under each letter as you pronounce and blend the sounds. Ask the children to repeat blending two or three times. Ask them to read the new word.

Erase the *i* and write an *e* on the board. Have children take away the *i* and put *e* in its place. Demonstrate blending and have the children repeat blending, following your example.

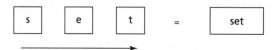

Ask, "What's the new word?"

6. Have the children take *s* away and put *p* in its place. Blend the sounds together in chorus. Ask, "Now what word have we made?"

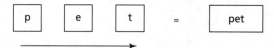

*Maze sentences—phonics in context.* Maze sentences have one word deleted and replaced by several choices. Make maze sentences from familiar reading material by deleting a word and then writing two or three choices that differ in the phonics patterns children are learning. Examples of maze sentences for words spelled with the r-controlled pattern include:

Mark wore a blue _____ to the party.
             (short, shirt)

Tom saw a _____ in the treetop.
            (bird, bark)

*Letter–sound T-charts.* These charts are another way of sorting words according to letter–sound patterns. In order to sort, children must identify the patterns they are learning.

| Short Vowel *can* | Silent *e* Long Vowel *cane* |
|---|---|
| lap | made |
| pot | time |
| sip | cube |
| dog | hope |
| cup | like |

*Build words.* Word building gives children practice applying letter–sound patterns. Children think about and reflect on patterns as they build words. Have children spell words with contrasting letter patterns; for example, have them spell *can* and *cane* or *boat* followed by *bat*. This type of compare-contrast building calls attention to how patterns are formed and represent sounds. Ask children to spell patterns they confuse when reading or spelling.

*Phonics word wall.* A phonics word wall has words grouped according to shared letter–sound patterns. Have children find and read words spelled with the patterns they are learning. A phonics word wall for the oi and ou diphthongs might look like:

| oi words | | ou words | |
|---|---|---|---|
| boil | point | about | mouse |
| coin | soil | count | our |
| join | spoil | found | out |
| moist | voice | house | round |
| noise | | loud | shout |

## Informal Assessment in the Classroom

Observe children as they use phonics to read and spell. Children who use the rimes and letter–sound patterns you have taught to sound out words and to spell are moving along nicely. Take a closer look at children who:

1. guess words without thinking about the letter–sounds,
2. associate the wrong sounds with rime or letter–sound patterns,
3. skip unfamiliar words, or
4. use only the beginning and ending letter–sounds when they have been taught vowel letter–sounds.

*Running records.* Use the miscues from running records to learn more about the letter–sound patterns the child knows and uses and the patterns the child misidentifies. Consider the letter–sound match between the correct word and the miscue. Look for letter–sound patterns the child routinely misidentifies. Only pay attention to patterns you have taught and expect the child to use. Disregard patterns that have not been taught. Reteach and give the child guided practice reading and spelling words with patterns you have taught and the child is not using. Table 2–4 is a checklist of possible misidentifications to guide you in evaluating misidentified patterns.

Sometimes children make careless mistakes because they race through text. This type of miscue is not rooted in a lack of decoding knowledge, but rather in a lack of attention to meaning and the absence of self-monitoring. Slow children down; insist that they read accurately and read words that make sense. Also teach children to monitor their own comprehension, to focus on meaning, and to self-correct when necessary.

*Informal phonics assessment.* Ask the child to read words with the letter–sound patterns the child should know and use. The informal assessment in Table 2–5 has nonsense words, not real words. The nonsense words represent all the major letter–sound patterns. Real words are not in these lists because the child may read some of them by sight. Nonsense words give us a better understanding of the child's phonics knowledge because the child has to sound them out. One letter is changed in each real word to make the nonsense words. Group 1 consists of nonsense words spelled with all the major vowel patterns: VC, VCe, VV, diphthongs (ow, ou, oi, oy), r-controlled and the au, aw, ew and ue patterns. Group 2 consists of beginning consonant blends; group 3 ending consonant blends; group 4 consonant digraphs. Check the words the child misidentifies. Reteach these patterns and give the child practice under your guidance reading and writing words with the patterns. Use the phonics checklist in Table 2–6 to keep track of the child's developing letter–sound knowledge.

**TABLE 2–4  Using Miscues to Identify the Phonics Patterns Children Need to Learn and Use**

Material:

1. One or more copies of a recent running record.

2. The text the child read.

3. Guide for recording misidentified patterns.

Directions:

1. Look at substitutions  and mispronunciations. Compare miscues with the correct word. Identify the letter–sound patterns in the misread word. Put a hash mark in the row that corresponds to the letter–sound pattern the child misidentified.

2. The child may misidentify more than one pattern in a word. Record all misidentified patterns.

3. Refer to Tables 2–1 and 2–2 for guidance in recognizing letter–sound patterns.

4. Compare the patterns misidentified with the patterns you have taught. Focus only on the patterns the child should know and use.

5. Reteach and provide guided practice reading and writing words spelled with patterns the child misidentified the most.

Examples:

| Correct Word | Miscue | Pattern |
|---|---|---|
| *ride* | *rid* | VCe pattern (magic *e*) |
| *hard* | *had* | *r*-controlled vowel pattern |
| *slid* | *slide* | VCe pattern |
| *street* | *stet* | V V long vowel pattern; consonant blend |

The child misidentified two vowel patterns in the last VCe and V V long vowel patterns examples.  The child read *stet* for *street*. If you notice that this child misidentifies many long vowel patterns but no other consonant blends, assume the miscued blend is a consequence of confusion identifying the long vowel. Further classroom observations will reveal whether the child knows and uses consonant blends.

Notice, too, that this child read *had* for *hard*. If you have taught the r-controlled vowel pattern, then you need to know whether this mistake was due to carelessness or to a lack of knowledge. You will determine this when you observe the child reading and writing throughout the school day. Overlooking and misspelling r-controlled words suggests that this child needs more instruction and more teacher-guided practice reading and writing words spelled with this pattern.

**Guidance for Using Miscues to Identify the Phonics Patterns Children Need to Learn and Use**

Name: _____

Date: _____

Leveled book: _____

| Does the child. . . | Yes/No | If yes, you may wish to use this space to write the misidentified patterns (rows 3 through 7). |
|---|---|---|
| 1. skip words? | | |
| 2. use only the beginning and/or ending letter–sound when you have taught one or more vowel patterns? | | |
| 3. misread or mispronounce blends (*cr, st, bl*, for example)? | | |
| 4. mispronounce consonant digraphs (*sh, ch, ph, th*, for example)? | | |
| 5. mistake long vowel words for short vowel words (reads *can* for *cane*)? | | |
| 6. misread diphthongs (*oy, oi, ou, ow*)? | | |
| 7. misread *r*-controlled words (*ar, er, ir, or, ur*)? | | |

## TABLE 2–5  Informal Phonics Assessment

**Directions to the child:**

I am going to show you some made-up words. Read each made-up word. Read the words across each line like this (sweep your finger under the words in the first line).

### Group 1

| | | | | | |
|---|---|---|---|---|---|
| 1. | lan | fet | mid | vop | sut |
| 2. | nate | nete | nipe | nobe | nube |
| 3. | lail | loat | tay | teap | feep |
| 4. | fey | fow | foud | foin | foy |
| 5. | marn | mer | mirt | mork | murn |
| 6. | daul | daw | lew | tue | |

### Group 2

| | | | | | |
|---|---|---|---|---|---|
| 1. | blup | clim | flut | glod | plig |
| 2. | slint | brog | crub | drig | frig |
| 3. | gran | prid | trup | sciff | smill |
| 4. | snup | sput | stog | swit | twag |

### Group 3

| | | | | |
|---|---|---|---|---|
| fict | moft | pold | selp | milt |
| fump | binch | pend | bink | fent |
| fept | lesk | clisp | rast | |

### Group 4

| | | | | |
|---|---|---|---|---|
| chot | phine | shup | thas | whit |
| cutch | | | | |

### Teacher's Guide

Ask the child to read the following nonsense words. We use nonsense words to make sure that the child does not read the words by sight. One letter is changed in real words to make nonsense words. The real word is shown in parenthesis. Check nonsense words the child reads correctly; write mispronunciations on the lines provided.

### Group 1

#### Short Vowels

| lan (man) | fet (let) | mid (did) | vop (mop) | sut (nut) |
|---|---|---|---|---|
| _____ | _____ | _____ | _____ | _____ |

#### Long Vowels

#### VCe

| nate (late) | nete (Pete) | nipe (ripe) | nobe (robe) | nube (cube) |
|---|---|---|---|---|
| _____ | _____ | _____ | _____ | _____ |

#### VV Pattern

| lail (mail) | loat (boat) | tay (day) | teap (leap) | feep (peel) |
|---|---|---|---|---|
| _____ | _____ | _____ | _____ | _____ |

fey (key)

_____

#### Diphthongs

**ow, ou, oi, oy**

fow (cow or long o as in mow)        If the child says "fow" as in mow, ask the child to say the word another way.

_____                                    _____

| foud (loud) | foin (coin) | foy (boy) |
|---|---|---|
| _____ | _____ | _____ |

**TABLE 2–5** (*Continued*)

*r-*Controlled

| marn (barn) | mer (her) | mirt (dirt) | mork (fork) | murn (burn) |
|---|---|---|---|---|
| _____ | _____ | _____ | _____ | _____ |

**au, aw**                                    **eu, ew**

| daul (haul) | daw (claw) | lew (new) | tue (true) |
|---|---|---|---|
| _____ | _____ | _____ | _____ |

## Consonants

These words are spelled with the consonant clusters and digraphs. The vowels are changed to make nonsense words.

### Group 2

**Consonant Clusters (also called consonant blends)**

*Ll* Clusters

| blup (blip) | clim (clam) |
|---|---|
| _____ | _____ |
| flut (flat) | glod (glad) |
| _____ | _____ |
| plig (plug) | slint (slant) |
| _____ | _____ |

*Rr* Clusters

| brog (brag) | crub (crab) |
|---|---|
| _____ | _____ |
| drig (drag) | frig (frog) |
| _____ | _____ |
| gran (grin) | prid (prod) |
| _____ | _____ |
| trup (trap) | |
| _____ | |

*Ss* Clusters

| sciff (scuff) | smill (small) |
|---|---|
| _____ | _____ |
| snup (snap) | sput |
| _____ | _____ |
| stog (stag) | |
| _____ | |

*Ww* Clusters

| swit (swat) | tway (twig) |
|---|---|
| _____ | _____ |

**TABLE 2–5  (Continued)**

**Group 3**

Final Clusters

| | |
|---|---|
| fict (fact) | moft (soft) |
| _____ | _____ |
| pold (told) | selp (help) |
| _____ | _____ |
| milt (malt) | fump (dump) |
| _____ | _____ |
| binch (bunch) | pend (pond) |
| _____ | _____ |
| bink (pink) | fent (went) |
| _____ | _____ |
| fept (kept) | lesk (desk) |
| _____ | _____ |
| clisp (clasp) | rast (fast) |
| _____ | _____ |

**Group 4**

Consonant Diagraphs

| | | |
|---|---|---|
| chot (chat) | phine (phone) | shup (ship) |
| _____ | _____ | _____ |
| thas (this) | whit (what) | cutch (catch) |
| _____ | _____ | _____ |

**TABLE 2–6  Phonics Checklist**

Child's Name _____         Date _____

Check each pattern the child uses to sound out and spell new words.

**Consonants**

**Single Consonants**

| | | | |
|---|---|---|---|
| _____ b (bat) | | _____ n (name) | |
| _____ c (cat) | | _____ m (mail) | |
| _____ c (city) | | _____ p (paint) | |
| _____ d (dog) | | _____ qu (queen) | |
| _____ f (fat) | | _____ r (ring) | |
| _____ g (goat) | | _____ s (sun) | |
| _____ g (gem) | | _____ t (top) | |
| _____ h (hat) | | _____ v (vat) | |
| _____ j (jam) | | _____ w (wagon) | |
| _____ k (kite) | | _____ x (extra) | |
| _____ l (lamp) | | _____ y (yellow) | |
| | | _____ z (zebra) | |

**TABLE 2.6** (*Continued*)

### Digraphs

**Beginning Digraphs**

_____ ch (chicken)

_____ ph (phone)

_____ sh (show)

_____ th (that)

_____ th (thing)

_____ wh (what)

_____ tch (catch)

**Final Digraphs**

_____ ch (lunch)

_____ ph (graph)

_____ sh (dish)

_____ th (bath)

_____ dg (edge)

_____ ck (deck)

### Consonant Clusters (Blends)

**Beginning Clusters**

*Ll* Clusters

_____ bl (black)      _____ cl (close)      _____ fl (flow)

_____ gl (glass)      _____ pl (plate)      _____ sl (slip)

*Rr* Clusters

_____ br (brown)      _____ cr (cross)      _____ dr (drop)

_____ fr (free)       _____ gr (greet)      _____ pr (pretty)

*Ss* Clusters

_____ sc (scout)      _____ sk (skirt)      _____ sm (small)

_____ sn (snack)      _____ sp (spell)      _____ st (stop)

_____ scr (scrap)     _____ spl (splash)    _____ spr (spring)

*Ww* Clusters

_____ dw (dwell)      _____ sw (swing)      _____ tw (twist)

**Final Clusters**

_____ ct (fact)       _____ nd (end)

_____ ft (lift)       _____ nk (pink)

_____ ld (old)        _____ nt (went)

_____ lk (milk)       _____ pt (kept)

_____ lp (help)       _____ sk (desk)

_____ lt (salt)       _____ sp (grasp)

_____ mp (jump)       _____ st (first)

_____ nch (lunch)

### Hard Sound of *cc* and *gg*

*ca, co, cu*

_____ ca (cat)

_____ co (cot)

_____ cu (cut)

*ga, go, gu*

_____ ga (gate)

_____ go (goat)

_____ gu (gum)

### Soft Sound of *cc* and *gg*

*ce, ci, cu*

_____ ce (cent)

_____ ci (city)

_____ cy (cycle)

*ge, gi, gy*

_____ ge (gem)

_____ gi (giant)

_____ gy (gym)

**TABLE 2.6  (Continued)**

**Silent Letters**

_____ bt (doubt)            _____ lk (chalk)

_____ ght (light)           _____ mb (comb)

_____ gn (gnaw, align)      _____ tch (witch)

_____ kn (know)             _____ wr (write)

VOWELS

**Short Vowels**

**CVC Pattern**

_____ a (cat)

_____ e (pet)

_____ i (sit)

_____ o (pot)

_____ u (bug)

**Long Vowels**

| **VCe Pattern** | **VV Pattern** | **CV Pattern** |
|---|---|---|
| _____ VCe (made) | _____ ai (train) | _____ (ta) (ta/ble) |
| _____ VCe (hide) | _____ oa (boat) | |
| _____ VCe (home) | _____ ay (play) | |
| _____ VCe (cube) | _____ ea (dream) | |
| | _____ ee (feet) | |
| | _____ ey (key) | |

**_r_-Controlled Vowels**

_____ ar (arm)             _____ ir (bird)           _____ ur (fur)

_____ er (her)             _____ or (corn)

**Diphthongs**

_____ ow (cow)             _____ oi (boil)

_____ ou (cloud)           _____ oy (boy)

**_oo_**

_____ oo (cook)            _____ oo (cool)

**_au, aw, al, all_**

_____ au (haul)

_____ aw (lawn)

_____ al (almost)

_____ all (tall)

**_eu, ew_**

_____ ew (new)

_____ ue (blue)

## PHONICS IN THE CLASSROOM

**Figure 2–14**
Brett's Story

### Kindergarten

Kindergarten classroom programs establish the foundation for the phonics taught in the first and second grades. Kindergarten teachers may spend about a half an hour to teach phonemic awareness, letter names, letter–sounds, word-family rimes, and high-frequency words, although many kindergarten teachers spend more time than this. Kindergarten teachers integrate phonics (and phonemic awareness) throughout the day and across subjects and experiences, so kindergartners really get much more than 30 minutes of instruction.

Kindergartners learn one sound for each letter and the letter names. At the beginning of the year, some kindergartners may use letterlike forms or random letters to write, as we see in Brett's story in Figure 2–14. Brett understands that letters go from left to right and is developing an awareness of punctuation.

Anna (Figure 2–15) knows some, but not all, the sounds associated with letters. When Anna spells, she says words softly to herself, listens for sounds, and writes a letter for the sounds she hears. Anna, like some kindergartners at the end of the year, writes a beginning and/or ending sound for each word. Anna uses the beginning and/or ending letter–sounds, picture clues, and story context cues to read new words. She also remembers some words by sight.

Kindergarten programs vary considerably. Some teach only letter names and a sound for each letter; others introduce a few word-family words. By the end of year, children in these classrooms know a name and sound for each letter, write a few words, know a handful of words by sight, and are familiar with a few word families.

**Figure 2–15**
Anna's Story

1. *Teach children to pay attention to all the letter–sound patterns in words.* Children at risk are apt to use only part of the letter–sound clues in a new word. Activities like Trading Letters (2.10) help children pay attention to all the letter–sounds and improve decoding, phonemic awareness, and comprehension (McCandliss, Beck, Sandak, & Perfetti, 2003).

2. *Make sure phonics instruction is systematic and intense.* Systematic, intensive phonics instruction narrows the gap between at-risk and average readers (Torgesen, Alexander, Wagner, Rachotte, Voeler, & Conway, 2001).

3. *Combine phonics with reading-connected text.* Children at risk will improve when you combine phonics and comprehension in the same program (Berninger et al., 2003; Blachman et al., 2004).

4. *Say the sounds aloud while decoding.* Phonics has a large oral language component. Saying the sounds aloud while decoding gives the at-risk child practice hearing, seeing, and saying sounds.

5. *Use some decodable text.* Give readers practice applying phonics while reading by having them read a few books with decodable words (Vadasy, Sanders, & Peyton, 2005).

## First Grade

First-grade teachers introduce vowel and consonant patterns and give children opportunities to use their developing phonics knowledge to read and write. Teachers may spend about a half hour each day directly teaching phonics, phonemic awareness, spelling, and high-frequency words. As the year progresses, teachers spend less time teaching phonemic awareness which leaves more instructional time to focus on phonics and spelling.

There is no solid research evidence to guide our decision on what to teach first. Therefore, first- (and second-) grade classroom programs vary in the specific letter patterns they teach. First-grade teachers may introduce consonant digraphs, such as *th*, *ch*, *sh*, *wh*, and *ck*; two-letter consonant blends, such as *bl* and *tr*, common word families, as well as short- and long-vowel patterns. Some programs introduce *r*-controlled vowels (*car*, *fur*) and diphthongs (*ou*, *ow*, *oi*, *oy*). First graders spell known words conventionally, self-monitor, correct miscues, and use letter–sound patterns along with the context and picture clues to identify new words in text.

Cheyenne (Figure 2–16) is a first grader who conventionally spells *I*, *won*, *a*, *fish*, *my*, *mom*, *win*, *it*, *like*, *the*, and *was*. All other words are spelled phonetically or inventively. We can read these words because Cheyenne writes a letter for each sound, as we see in *golld* for *gold*, *hilpt* for *helped*, and *fier* for *fair*. Decoding is slow and time-consuming. However, by the end of the first grade Cheyenne will be a faster and more accurate decoder. At this point Cheyenne benefits from learning how different letter combinations represent long- and short-vowel sounds, as shown in Table 2–2.

Maryanne (Figure 2–17) knows more words and is faster at decoding. She enjoys playing on the monkey bars (*mucey bras*) at school, as she tells us in her story. While children like Cheyenne and Maryanne cannot read silently, they can read orally and hence benefit from developing oral reading fluency (explained in chapter 5). All things considered, kindergartners and first graders get a healthy dose of phonics. Most first graders do not get enough practice decoding and spelling words to master all the phonics information they need, which brings us to the second grade.

**Figure 2–16**
Cheyenne's Story

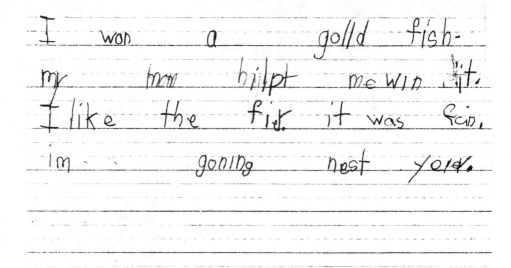

## Second Grade

Second graders are expected to use phonics and word structure (explained in chapter 3) to decode two-syllable words in text. Children self-monitor and correct miscues. Second-grade teachers may spend approximately 25 minutes or so teaching phonics, spelling, and word structure each day, depending on children's development as readers. Most second-grade classroom programs revisit and review the patterns introduced in the first grade and introduce any patterns that have not been previously introduced. Second-grade programs introduce the less frequently occurring vowel patterns of *au*, *aw*, *ew*, and *ue*. Added to this, children may also learn three-letter consonant clusters (*spr* and *spl*, for example), silent consonants like *wr* and *kn*, the two sounds of *g* and *c*, and the diphthongs (*oi*, *oy*, *ow*, *ou*), if these patterns were not introduced in the first grade. Second graders conventionally spell the words they can read.

Peter (Figure 2–18) is in the second half of second grade. In second grade he will fully master all the patterns in Tables 2–1 and 2–2. At present he knows long- and short-vowel patterns and is now refining his knowledge of diphthongs as well as *r*-controlled and other patterns, like *aw* and *au*. An average second grader like Peter will go

**Figure 2–17**
Maryanne's Story

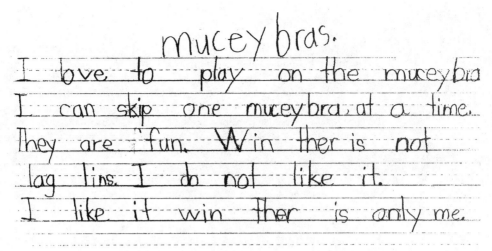

mucey bras.
I love to play on the muceybra
I can skip one muceybra at a time.
They are fun. Win ther is not
lag lins. I do not like it.
I like it win ther is only me.

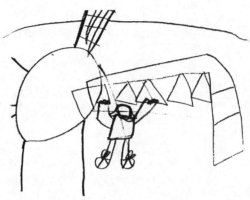

**Figure 2–18**
Peter's Story

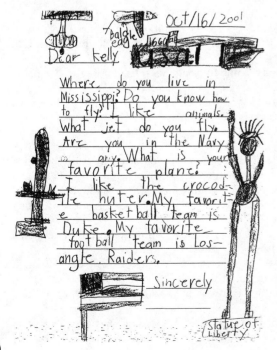

to third grade with enough phonics knowledge and enough ability to use context to learn words independently.

## Third Grade

Third-grade classroom reading programs refine the phonics skills and strategies developed in the earlier grades. Third-grade teachers may spend about 15 minutes each day teaching phonics, word structure (chapter 3), and spelling, depending on children's development as readers and the priorities of the program itself. Although teachers review the letter–sound patterns taught in first and second grade, phonics is not the primary emphasis. Word structure (chapter 3) is stressed because third graders need this knowledge in order to read complex words with prefixes and suffixes.

## Fourth, Fifth, and Sixth Grades

Because fourth through sixth graders are skilled at using phonics and because the words in their texts are complex, fourth-, fifth-, and sixth-grade classroom programs focus on teaching the structure of long words (explained in chapter 3). However, phonics is reviewed through spelling lessons in which children spell words with the phonics patterns learned in previous years.

# REFERENCES

Araujo, L. (2002). The literacy development of kindergarten English-language learners. *Journal of Research in Childhood Education, 16*, 232–247.

Berninger, V. W., Vermeulen, K., Abbott, R. D., McCutchen, D., Cotton, S., Cude, J., Dorn, S., & Sharon, T. (2003). Comparison of three approaches to supplementary reading instruction for low-achieving second-grade readers. *Language, Speech, and Hearing Services in Schools, 34*, 101–116.

Blachman, B. A., Schatschneider, C., Fletcher, J. M., Francis, D. J., Clonan, S. M., Shaywitz, B. A., & Shaywitz, S. E. (2004). Effects of intensive reading remediation for second and third graders and a 1-year follow-up study. *Journal of Educational Psychology, 96*, 444–461.

Chiappe, P., Siegel, L. S., & Wade-Woolley, L. (2002). Linguistic diversity and the development of reading skills: A longitudinal study. *Scientific Studies of Reading, 6*, 369–400.

Christensen, C. A., & Bowey, J. A. (2005). The efficacy of orthographic rime, grapheme-phoneme correspondences, and implicit phonics approaches to teaching decoding skills. *Scientific Studies of Reading, 9*, 327–340.

Denton, C. A., Anthony, J. L., Parker, R., & Hasbrouck, J. E. (2004). Effects of two tutoring programs on the English reading development of Spanish-English bilingual students. *The Elementary School Journal, 104*, 289–305.

Ehri, L. C. (2000). Learning to read and learning to spell: Two sides of a coin. *Topics in Language Disorders, 20*, 19–36.

Ehri, L. C. (2004). Teaching phonemic awareness and phonics: An explanation of the national reading panel meta-analysis. In P. McCardle & V. Chhabra (Eds.), *The voice of evidence in reading research* (pp. 153–186). Baltimore, MD: Paul H. Brookes Publishing.

Eldredge, J. L. (2005). Foundations of fluency: An exploration. *Reading Psychology, 26*, 161–181.

Gunn, B., Smolkowski, K., Biglan, A., & Black, C. (2002). Supplemental instruction in decoding skill for Hispanic and Non-Hispanic students in early elementary school: A follow-up. *Journal of Special Education, 36*, 69–79.

Johnston, R. S., & Watson, J. (2004). Accelerating the development of reading, spelling, and phoneme awareness skills in initial readers. *Reading and Writing: An Interdisciplinary Journal, 17*, 327–357.

Lesaux, N. K., & Siegel, L. S. (2003). The development of reading in children who speak English as a second language. *Developmental Psychology, 39*, 1005–1019.

McCandliss, B., Beck, I. L., Sandak, R., & Perfetti, C. (2003). Focusing on attention to decoding for children with poor reading skills: Design and preliminary tests of the word building intervention. *Scientific Studies of Reading, 7*, 75–104.

National Reading Panel (2000). *Report of the national reading panel: Teaching children to read: An evidence-based assessment of the scientific research literature on reading and its implications for reading instruction: Reports of subgroups* (NIH Publication no. 00–4754). Washington, DC: U.S. Government Printing Office.

Otaiba, S. A. (2005). How effective is code-based reading tutoring in English for English language learners and preservice teacher-tutors? *Remedial and Special Education, 26*, 245–254.

Rupley, W. H., Rodriquez, M., Mergen, S. L., Willson, V. L., & Nichols, W. D. (2000). Effects of structural features on word recognition development of Hispanic and non-Hispanic second graders. *Reading and Writing: An Interdisciplinary Journal, 13*, 337–2000.

Schatschneider, C., Fletcher, J. M., Francis, D. J., Carlson, C. S., & Foorman, B. R. (2004). Kindergarten prediction of reading skills: A longitudinal comparative analysis. *Journal of Educational Psychology, 96*, 265–282.

Schwanenflugel, P. J., Hamilton, A. M., Kuhn, M. R., Wisenbaker, J. M., & Stahl, S. A. (2004). Becoming a fluent reader: Reading skill and prosodic features in the oral reading of young readers. *Journal of Educational Psychology, 96*, 119–129.

Stuart, M. (2004). Getting ready for reading: A follow-up study of inner city second language learners at the end of Key Stage I. *British Journal of Educational Psychology, 74*, 15–36.

Torgesen, J. K., Alexander, A. W., Wagner, R. K., Rashotte, C. A., Voeller, K. K. S., & Conway, T. (2001). Intensive remedial instruction for children with severe reading disabilities: Immediate and long-term outcomes from two instructional approaches. *Journal of Learning Disabilities, 78*, 33–58.

Vadasy, P. E., Sanders, E. A., & Peyton, J. A. (2005). Relative effectives of reading practice or word-level instruction in supplemental tutoring: How text matters. *Journal of Learning Disabilities, 38*, 364–380.

# 3

# DECODING WITH
# STRUCTURAL ANALYSIS

There are 28 variations on the word *use* in the following table. Can you add to the list? At least four words are missing. (The answer is at the end of this chapter.)

| prefix + *use* | *use* + suffix | | prefix + *use* + suffix | |
|---|---|---|---|---|
| reuse | used | useful | reused | overused |
| disuse | user | using | reuses | overuses |
| multiuse | uses | useless | unused | reusable |
| overuse | users | usefully | misused | overusing |
| | usage | uselessly | misuses | unusable |
| | usable | usefulness | underused | misusing |

Structural analysis is a strategy for reading complex words. Children use structural analysis to divide words into different parts that represent (1) meaning and sound (*rest-less* = rest/less) or (2) only sound (*proportion* = pro/por/tion).

## STRUCTURAL ANALYSIS
## CONTRIBUTES TO VOCABULARY AND FLUENCY

Complex words are far more prevalent in the harder books read by third, fourth, fifth and sixth graders than in books for beginning readers. As word length increases children must look beyond the rather small letter–sound patterns of phonics to identify the large, multiletter chunks in complex words. Structural analysis serves the same function in third through sixth grades as phonics in kindergarten through second grade. When readers use structural analysis they combine phonics letter–sound patterns into large, multiletter chunks. Children then use this knowledge to decode and learn the complex words that are so common in story and information text beyond the early grades.

Structural analysis makes it possible for the child to read compound words (*baseball*) and contractions (*can't*) as single units. The child recognizes prefixes (*precook*),

---

**BEST PRACTICES FOR EFFECTIVE TEACHING**

1. *Use clue words.* Clue words—words that prompt memory—illustrate patterns and help readers remember the patterns. Use children's suggestions or make a list yourself, such as *pencil (pen/cil)* for a closed syllable or *candle (can/dle)* for the Cle syllable.

2. *Make sure children know how to read the base word (fill) before asking them to* decode the word with a prefix or suffix *(refilled).* If children cannot automatically read base words, then children will not be able to readily locate prefixes and suffixes.

3. *Teach meaning families.* Group words with the same Greek or Latin word families that call attention to word meaning (*aud-* family as in *auditory, audition,* and *audio*).

---

suffixes (*read<u>ing</u>*), and Greek and Latin roots (*tele<u>phone</u>* and *<u>phon</u>ic*) as meaningful word parts. When a new word doesn't have meaningful parts, the good reader divides it into syllables that, when blended together, yield the pronunciation of the word (*cam/er/a*).

Understanding word structure helps the child infer word meaning. Inferring word meaning helps the child learn new words. A larger reading vocabulary, in turn, contributes to fluency and comprehension. The more words the child instantly recognizes and understands, the better the fluency (Eldredge, 2005).

Structural analysis is particularly suited for reading complex words in the upper grades. When a word is divided into multiletter parts (*ma/lig/nant*), there are fewer units to blend than when analyzing a word into phonics letter patterns. With fewer units to blend word identification is faster. When the word parts themselves give the child insight into word meaning, adding new words to the child's reading vocabulary becomes much more efficient. The child who recognizes many word parts has a larger reading vocabulary and better comprehension than the child who recognizes few word parts (Deacon & Kirby, 2004; Nagy, Berninger, & Abbott, 2006).

## THE STRUCTURE OF COMPLEX WORDS

For the purposes of teaching reading, we will divide the structure of words into five multiletter word parts: (1) compound words, (2) contractions, (3) prefixes and suffixes, (4) Greek and Latin roots, and (5) syllables.

### Compound Words

Compound words are two words glued together to form a single word, such as *base + ball = baseball.* The meaning of some compound words is quite similar to the two words individually, as in *barefoot* and *campfire.* If children know the meaning of the individual words that make up this type of compound, they can infer the meaning of the compound itself. The meaning of other compounds has little connection to the meaning of the two words. For instance, *butter* and *cup* do not suggest the meaning of *buttercup.* Children might assume they know the meaning of *buttercup* because *butter* and *cup* are familiar words. To understand compounds like *buttercup,* children must look beyond the individual words to consider sentence context and prior knowledge. You will need to directly teach the meaning of these compound words if the sentence context does not give enough clues to meaning.

## Contractions

A contraction is a single word formed by combining two words. We use an apostrophe to represent missing letters (*is not = isn't*). In English, we abbreviate the second word in a contraction. In order to read and write contractions, children must understand the basic concept behind using the apostrophe and know the difference between an apostrophe that indicates an abbreviated word (*wasn't*) and an apostrophe that shows possession (*Jane's* book). Word meaning is the same whether words are written separately or as contractions.

## Prefixes and Suffixes

Prefixes are added to the beginning of words (*re + play = replay*); suffixes are added to the end (*play + ing = playing*). Prefixes change meaning (*un + happy = unhappy*) or make meaning more specific (*re + play = replay*). The suffixes *-es/s, -ed, -ing, -er* and *-est*, called inflected endings, change the number (*cats*) or the verb tense (*played*) or indicate a comparison (*bigger*). Other suffixes affect meaning and grammatical usage. Children who understand the effect of prefixes and suffixes on word meaning have better comprehension (Carlisle, 2000) and are better spellers than children who do not have this knowledge (Leong, 2000). Table 3–1 is a list of the most common prefixes and suffixes in Grades 3 through 9.

**TABLE 3–1  The Most Common Prefixes and Suffixes in Grades 3 Through 9**[*]

Prefixes and Suffixes that Occur in Up to 82 Percent of Affixed Words

| Prefixes | Suffixes |
|---|---|
| un-, re- | -s (-es), -ed, -ing, -ly |
| in-, im-, ir-, il- (not) | -er and –or (agent) |
| dis-, en-, em-, non- | -ion, -tion, -ation, ition |
| in- and im- (meaning into) | -able and –ible |
| over- (meaning too much) | |
| mis-, sub-, pre- | |

Prefixes and Suffixes that Occur in 18 Percent or Less of Affixed Words

| Prefixes | Suffixes |
|---|---|
| inter-, fore- | -al and –ial (capable of) |
| de-, trans-, super- | -y, -ness, -ity, and –ty |
| semi-, anti-, mid- | -ment, -ic |
| under- (too little) | -ous, -eous, and –ious |
| | -en, -er (comparative) |
| | -ive, -ative, -itive, -ful |
| | -less, -est |

[*] White, T. G., Sowell, J., & Yanagihara, A. (1989). "Teaching elementary students to use word part clues." *The Reading Teacher, 42,* 302–308.

Every child needs a plan to tackle long, complex words. One way to tackle a word with prefixes and/or suffixes is to "use your fingers" to cover these word parts. The Use Your Fingers strategy consists of these five easy steps:

**Use Your Fingers**

| | |
|---|---|
| **Step 1** | Do you see a prefix? Put your finger over the prefix. <br> *unbreakable – un = breakable* |
| **Step 2** | Do you see a suffix? Put your finger over the suffix. <br> *breakable – able = break* |
| **Step 3** | Read the word. <br> *break* |
| **Step 4** | Take your finger off the prefix. Read the word. <br> *unbreak = unbreak* |
| **Step 5** | Take your finger off the suffix. Read the whole word. <br> *unbreakable* |

## Greek and Latin Roots

Many English words include a word from the Greek or Latin languages. We call the borrowed portions root words. English words with the same root belong to a meaning family. For example, *magn-*, of Latin origin, means great. *Magnificent, magnify, magnitude*, and *magnanimous* are examples of words in the *magn-* meaning family. Grouping words into meaning families helps children identify roots and gives children insight into word meaning.

## Syllables

The syllable is the basic unit of pronunciation. Every English syllable has one and only one vowel sound. Syllables may have more than one vowel letter (rain), but never more than one vowel sound. Every vowel sound we hear in a word equals one syllable. This is true for short and long words alike.

In order to break long words into syllables children need to know which letters form syllables and which do not. Teach children to look for the following syllable patterns:

1. *Compound Word Syllable* Divide compounds between the two words ( *flash/light*).
2. *VC Closed Syllable* A closed syllable ends in a consonant sound and the vowel is usually short (*pen/cil*).
3. *CV Open Syllable* This syllable ends in a vowel sound and the vowel usually represents a long sound (*me, si/lent*). In words where one consonant is placed between two vowels, the consonant often goes with the second vowel.
4. *Cle Syllable Le* at the end of a word usually forms the last syllable. The consonant preceding the *le* typically begins the syllable (*han/dle*).
5. *VCCV Syllable* When two consonants are between two vowels the first syllable is often the VC closed syllable (*com/mand, per/fect*).
6. *Prefix and Suffix Syllables* Prefixes and suffixes usually represent separate syllables, with the exception of *-s/es* and *-ed* when the *-ed* is pronounced /t/, as in the word *equipped*.
7. *VCCCV Three-Letter Consonant Cluster and Digraph Syllables* If three consecutive consonants include a consonant cluster or digraph, try dividing the syllables either before or after the cluster (*ex/tra*) or digraph (*to/geth/er*).(See pages 79–83, "Informal Assessment or Additional Practices for Observing Developing Decoding with Structural Analysis")

# ACTIVITIES

## 17 ACTIVITIES TO DEVELOP DECODING WITH STRUCTURAL ANALYSIS

### 3.1   Illustrated Compounds

- Large group, small group, individual, or learning center
- Use to develop knowledge of compound words.

Children develop insight into compound words through illustrating word meaning.

**Material:** List of compounds; pencils, markers, or crayons.

**Step-by-step directions:**

1. Have children turn a piece of paper horizontally and write a compound word at the top and the two words individually at the bottom.
2. Children illustrate the meaning of the individual words and the compound word.
3. Children write a + between the two words and an = followed by the whole word (*bull + frog = bullfrog*), as shown in Figure 3–1.

**Figure 3–1**
Illustrated Compound Words

### 3.2   Create Your Own Compound

- Large group, small group, individual, or learning center
- Use to develop knowledge of compound words.

Children make their own compound words by gluing together two words and defining their creative compounds.

**Material:** Word cards; paper; pencils; crayons.

**Step-by-step directions:**

1. Children in a small group select two word cards from a face-down stack.
2. Each child puts the two words together to make a unique compound. Children may trade words with each other if they wish.

**Figure 3–2**
Create Your Own Compounds

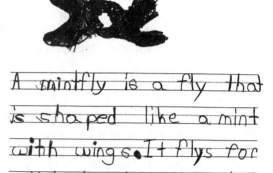

3. Each child writes the new compound word and makes up a definition, as shown in Figure 3–2.

---

## 3.3    Folding Contractions

- Small group
- Use to develop knowledge of contractions.

Children form contractions by using masking tape to hide deleted letters.

**Material:** Sentence strips; masking tape; marker.

**Step-by-step directions:**

1. Write the first word of a contraction to the left of the sentence strip. Write the second word immediately after the first word; do not leave a space between the words.
2. Write an apostrophe on a piece of masking tape.
3. Show the children how to fold the deleted letter behind the words. Tape the newly formed contraction together with an apostrophe.

---

## 3.4    Undoing Contractions

- Small group, individual, or learning center
- Use to develop knowledge of contractions.

**Figure 3–3**
Undoing
Contractions

Directions: Work with a partner.

Step 1. Read each contraction in the first column.

Step 2. In the second column write the first word that makes up the contraction.

Step 3. Write the second word in the last column.

Step 4. Look at the first contraction. It is done for you. This is an example of how to write your answers.

| Contraction | First Word | Second Word |
|---|---|---|
| isn't | is | not |
| I'm | | |
| she'll | | |
| we've | | |
| can't | | |
| they're | | |
| that's | | |
| shouldn't | | |
| haven't | | |
| would've | | |

Children separate contractions into the two original words.

**Material:** One undoing guide for each child (Figure 3–3).

**Step-by-step directions:**

1. Make three columns: Write contractions in first column. Leave the other columns blank. Label the first column Contraction, the second First Word, the third Second Word.

2. Children write the set of words that make up each contraction in the second and third columns. (Figure 3–3).

## 3.5 Prefix and Suffix Transparency Concentration

- Small group
- Use to develop knowledge of prefixes and suffixes.

This activity is just like the regular concentration word game, with one important exception: Words with prefixes and suffixes are written on an overhead transparency instead of on cards.

**Figure 3–4**
Prefix and Suffix
Transparency
Concentration

|   | 1 | 2 | 3 | 4 |
|---|---|---|---|---|
| A | Contentment | lively | happiness | joyous |
| B | Contentment | hoping | boastful | hopped |
| C | lively | happiness | joyous | boastful |
| D | resourceful | hoping | hopped | resourceful |

|   | 1 | 2 | 3 | 4 |
|---|---|---|---|---|
| A |  |  |  | joyous |
| B |  | hoping |  |  |
| C |  |  | joyous |  |
| D |  | hoping |  |  |

**Material:** Overhead transparencies with rows of words with prefixes or suffixes; small sticky notes to cover the words; as many colors of nonpermanent markers as there are children in a small group.

Make a square with an equal number of boxes. Write two words with a prefix or suffix randomly on a transparency. Write a numeral over each column and a capital letter beside each row. Cut small sticky notes in half. Cover the words with the sticky notes (Figure 3–4).

**Step-by-step directions:**

1. Divide a small group into two teams.
2. Alternating between teams, a child tells you the columns and row numbers of two sticky notes to remove.
3. The team earns one point for each correct match. Incorrect matches are covered again with sticky notes.

## 3.6    Sticky-Note Suffix Books

- Small group or learning center
- Use to develop knowledge of suffixes.

Children write words with suffixes on sticky notes and then put the sticky notes together to create sticky-note suffix books. Use this activity to give children practice with base words that change spelling when suffixes are added, such as *happily*; to practice adding *-s* (*plays*) and *-es* (*benches*); and to explore the suffixes added to the beginning of words.

**Figure 3–5**
Sticky-Note Suffix Book

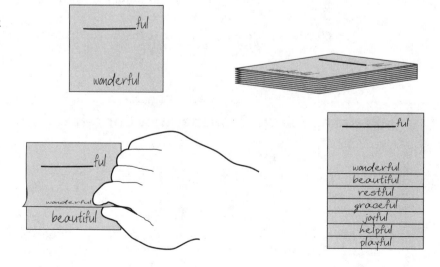

**Material:** Sticky notes; pencils; staplers; chart paper; marker; construction paper.

**Step-by-step directions:**

1. Write a suffix on a large sticky note.
2. Write base words with the suffix on smaller sticky notes (Figure 3–5). Staple the pages together.
3. Partners flip through their sticky-note books to read the words.

## 3.7    Suffix T-Charts

- Small group divided into pairs
- Use to develop knowledge of suffixes.

T-charts are a paper-and-pencil method of sorting words (Figure 3–6) according to whether words do or do not change spelling when suffixes are added.

**Material:** A T-chart for each pair.

**Step-by-step directions:**

1. Distribute a T-chart to each pair in the small group.
2. Children read the words in the list, decide which words do and do not change spelling, and write the words with the suffix (Figure 3–6).

**Figure 3–6**
Suffix T-Chart

Names: _Darla_____ ___Joe____

*Directions:*
Add ____-est____ to the base words: tall, happy, pretty, big, fat, ugly, short, fair, mean, loud, fast, green, round, hungry, weird, near, sweet, flat.

Write words with -est in Column A if the base word spelling <u>does not</u> change.
Write words with -est in Column B if the base word spelling <u>does</u> change.
The first one is already done.

| Column A | Column B |
|---|---|
| Base word + *est* | Base word + *est* |
| Base word spelling <u>does not</u> change. | Base word spelling <u>does</u> change. |
| tallest | happiest |
| shortest | prettiest |
| fairest | biggest |
| meanest | fattest |
| loudest | ugliest |
| fastest | hungriest |
| greenest | |
| weirdest | |
| nearest | |
| sweetest | |

## 3.8    Crossword Puzzles

- Pairs, individual, or learning center
- Use to develop knowledge of prefixes and suffixes.

Children solve crossword puzzles by identifying the prefixes and suffixes in words and writing the prefixes and suffixes in the correct blanks.

**Material:** Crossword puzzles (Figure 3–7); words with prefixes or suffixes the children are learning to read and write.

**Step-by-step directions:**

1. Children read the words under the columns *Across* and *Down* and identify the prefixes or suffixes in the words.
2. Children write *only* the prefixes or suffixes in the correct blanks. Figure 3–7 shows a suffix crossword puzzle.

**Figure 3–7**
Crossword Puzzle

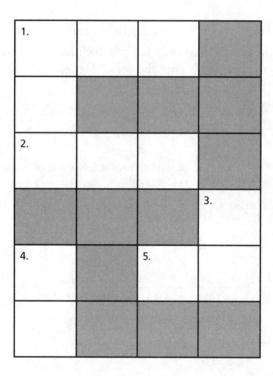

| Across | Down |
|--------|------|
| 1. sheepish | 1. active |
| 2. brightest | 3. longer |
| 5. stronger | 4. calmly |

## 3.9    Prefix, Suffix, or Root Webs

- Small group
- Use to develop knowledge of prefixes, suffixes, or Greek and Latin roots.

Children analyze semantic connections among words with the same prefixes, suffixes or Greek and Latin root words and create webs to illustrate these connections.

**Material:** Dictionaries; large chart paper; marker.

**Figure 3–8**
Web for -*ly* and *un*-

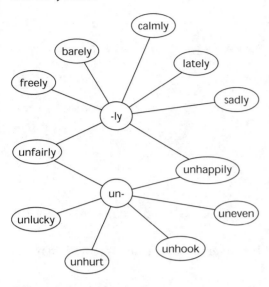

**Step-by-step directions:**

1. Ask small groups to focus on different prefixes, suffixes or root words. Have children make a list of words with the prefix, suffix, or Greek or Latin root they are learning.

2. Children write the prefix, suffix, or root in the center of a piece of paper and arrange words into a web that shows meaningful connections (Figure 3–8).

3. Ask children to connect the words in the web by drawing lines among the words.

4. Groups complete the webs by defining the meaning of the prefix or suffix at the bottom of the page.

## 3.10    Prefix and Suffix Slides

- Pairs, individual, or learning center
- Use to develop knowledge of prefixes or suffixes.

Children slide a poster board strip through slots to add suffixes to words (Figure 3–9).

**Material:** Poster board strips. For each word slice, cut poster board into one 2½- × 8-inch strip and one 3- × 10-inch strip. Cut slits in the 2½-inch strip as shown in Figure 3–9. Cut a slit toward the right to make a suffix slide, and to the left for a prefix slide. Write words or suffixes on each strip.

**Figure 3–9**
Prefix and Suffix Slides

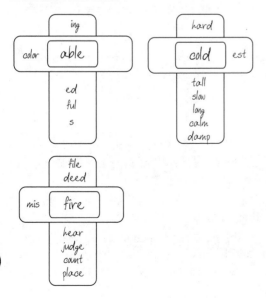

**Step-by-step directions:**

1. Pairs take turns sliding the strips to form words with prefixes or suffixes.

2. Place blank poster board strips in a learning center or distribute strips to individuals. Children work individually or in pairs to make their own slides. Have children write the words with prefixes or suffixes on paper before making the slides. Check the words for accuracy before children make slides.

3. Have children exchange the slides they make. Pass around the slides until everyone in the small group has had an opportunity to read the words on each slide.

## 3.11    Graffiti

- Large or small group
- Use to develop knowledge of prefixes, suffixes, or Greek and Latin root words.

Children write words with prefixes, suffixes, or Greek and Latin root words on a large chart.

**Material:** Large chart (butcher paper works well); colored markers.

**Step-by-step directions:**

1. Write two or three prefixes, suffixes, or Greek and Latin root words at the top of a piece of chart or butcher paper.
2. Fasten the paper to a bulletin board and leave a few colored markers nearby.
3. Children write words with the prefixes, suffixes, or Greek and Latin roots on the chart. Children may write words creatively and use any color so long as words are legible.
4. After a week have children find certain words on the chart, have children read the words in chorus, and add some of the words to the word wall in your classroom.

## 3.12    Syllable-by-Syllable Decoding

- Small group
- Use to develop knowledge of syllables.

Children find syllables in complex words on sentence strips and then use the syllables to pronounce the long words.

**Materials:** Sentence strips with complex words written on them; dictionaries; multiple copies of the books children are reading in your classroom.

**Step-by-step directions:**

1. Write a long word on a sentence strip, such as *explosion*. Read the word.
2. Take the end of the strip and gently fold it over so that only the first syllable, *ex-*, shows. Ask children to read the first syllable.
3. Reveal the second syllable, *plo-*, and ask children to read it. Then ask the children to read the two syllables together, *explo-*.
4. Unfold the strip to reveal the last syllable, *-sion*. Have children read the whole word, *explosion*. Examples of other long words for sentence-strip syllable reading include *enormous* (*e-*; *enor-*; *enormous*), *forgotten* ( *for-*; *forgot-*; *forgotten*), and *tolerate* (*tol-*; *toler-*; *tolerate*).

**TEACHING ENGLISH LANGUAGE LEARNERS**

1. *Teach word parts that are common to English and the child's home language.* Some of the prefixes, suffixes, and root words in English are used in other languages, particularly Romance languages like Spanish and French (Manzo, Manzo, & Thomas, 2006). Understanding how English and the home language are alike makes it possible for the child to generalize from the home language to English, keeps instruction meaning based, and honors the child's home language (Pérez Cañado, 2005).

2. *Teach structural analysis along with word meaning.* Emphasize word meaning when you teach English learners about the structure of English words. Point out words with structures you are teaching; ask children to explain how these word parts affect meaning.

## 3.13 Greek and Latin Root Trees

- Small group
- Use to develop knowledge of Greek and Latin roots.

**Material:** Construction paper tree trunks; construction paper treetops; marker. Cut construction paper to resemble tree trunks (select light tan, not dark brown). Write a Greek or Latin root and the meaning of each root on each trunk (Figure 3–10). Fasten the trunks and treetops to a bulletin board.

**Figure 3–10**
Greek and Latin
Root Trees

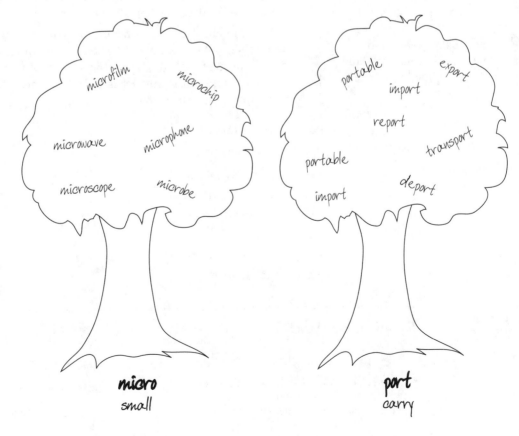

**Step-by-step directions:**

1. Discuss the Greek and Latin roots. Talk about how they give us some insight into word meaning.
2. Have children suggest a few Greek and Latin roots they have been learning. Write these roots and their meanings on the tree trunks.
3. Children find and then write words with the roots on leaves, which are then fastened to the proper tree (Figure 3–10).

## 3.14    Haiku

- Small group
- Use to develop knowledge of syllables.

Children explore syllables and meaning as they write haiku, a form of Japanese poetry that consists of words of no more than 17 syllables that are arranged in only three lines.

**Material:** Haiku poems; several pieces of large chart paper; markers; index cards; masking tape; haiku rules chart; colored construction paper; colored chalk or crayons.

**Step-by-step directions:**

1. Haiku written in English has three lines of 17 syllables arranged in a 5-7-5 syllable pattern.

**Figure 3–11**
Haiku

2. Select a theme and write a whole-group haiku poem. Count the syllables to make sure that the haiku follows the 5-7-5-syllable formula. A group of third graders wrote "After the Rain" (Figure 3–11) after a spring shower.

3. When the children are comfortable with haiku, ask them to write their own haiku poems. The first few times children write haiku, suggest that they write the subject of their poem on the first line, where the subject is found on the second line, and what the subject does on the third line.

---

After the Rain

Mushy, soggy mud
Blue jays chirping cheerfully
Cool, refreshing breeze

---

*How to Write a Haiku Poem*

Write only three lines.
Line one has five syllables.
Line two has seven syllables.
Line three has five syllables.
Haiku does not rhyme.
Do not use the words *like* or *as*.
Try to describe nature.

## 3.15    Syllable Football

- Pairs
- Use to develop knowledge of syllables.

This is a good activity for two children to practice making words with syllables.

**Material:** A football field divided in half, as shown in Figure 3–12; cards with syllables that begin and end words; a few blank cards.

**Step-by-step directions:**

1. Give two children a stack of cards with a syllable on each. Each child plays on one half of the football field.

2. Children take turns making words with the syllable cards, or writing syllables on blank cards to make two-syllable words. Each word is written on a line on the field (Figure 3–12).

3. Children may use the same syllables more than once. However, if a word is already on the football field, that word cannot be used again.

4. The object is to reach the goal post.

**Figure 3–12**
Syllable Football

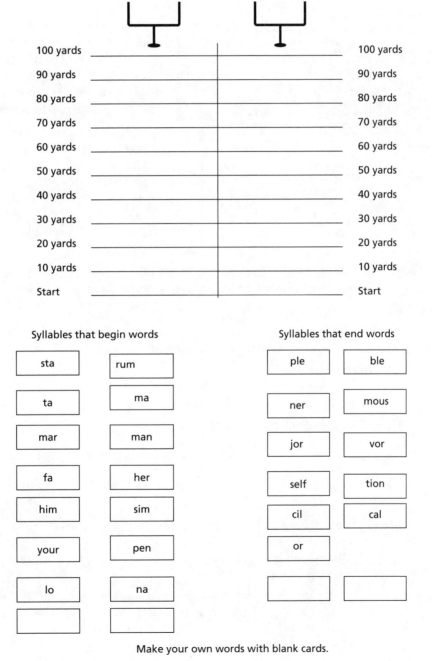

Make your own words with blank cards.

## 3.16   Syllable Strips

- Small group
- Use to develop knowledge of syllables.

Children tape words on long, colorful strips that have the same number of syllables.

**Material:** Long strips of colored butcher paper; small index cards or construction paper rectangles; marker; tape. Cut a different color butcher paper into a long strips. Make up to six strips, depending on children's development as readers. (You may use white butcher paper if colored is not available.)

**Figure 3–13**
Syllable Strips

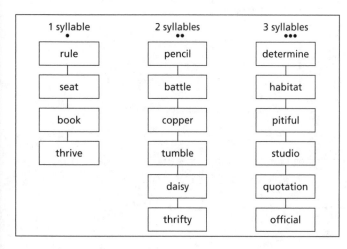

**Step-by-step directions:**

1. Write one dot at the top of one strip; two dots at the top of the second strip; and so on up to six dots. The dots indicate the number of syllables. Alternatively, you might simply write one syllable, two syllables, and three syllables at the top of each strip.

2. Give children index cards. Discuss how to identify the number of syllables in words. Children take turns pronouncing words and counting syllables. Children then tape the words to the syllable strips that have the number of dots (or title) that correspond to the number of syllables in words, as shown in Figure 3–13.

3. Make strips as long as you like. Children may later add to the syllable strips complex words that they read in storybooks and textbooks.

## 3.17   Syllable Boxes

- Small group, pairs, individual, or learning center
- Use to develop knowledge of syllables.

Children divide words into syllables and write syllables in syllable boxes (Figure 3–14).

**Material:** Boxes for the number of syllables in the multisyllable words children are reading.

**Step-by-step directions:**

1. Discuss syllable patterns and how to use these patterns to help pronounce complex words.

2. As the children watch, write a multisyllable word on the board. Then draw as many boxes joined together as there are syllables in a word. Demonstrate how to divide the word into syllables. Write each syllable in one box (Figure 3–14).

**Figure 3–14**
Syllable Boxes

*Directions*:
Read the words. Write the syllables in the boxes below the words.

rabbit             traveling              entertaining

| | |     | | | |     | | | | |

(Answers)

| rab | bit |     | tra | vel | ing |     | en | ter | tain | ing |

planet             sandwich           third

| | |     | | |     | |

(Answers)

| plan | et |     | sand | wich |     | third |

3.  Ask individuals or pairs to divide complex words into syllables and write the syllables in the boxes.

4.  Have individuals or pairs find three other long words, make boxes for those words, and write the syllables in boxes. Then have children rewrite the three words on a blank piece of paper and draw boxes under the words. Ask children to write their names on the back of the paper.

5.  Collect papers. Distribute the three new words, taking care to give each individual or pair a copy of words they did not turn in.

6.  After the children complete the three syllables created by their peers, invite a few volunteers to write their multisyllable words and syllable boxes on the board. Discuss the syllable patterns and how finding syllables helps us pronounce long words.

## INFORMAL ASSESSMENT OR ADDITIONAL PRACTICES FOR OBSERVING AND DEVELOPING DECODING WITH STRUCTURAL ANALYSIS

### Additional Practices

*Slash syllables.* Ask children to put slashes between the syllables of complex words you have written on the board. This gives children practice finding syllables under your guidance and also gives you information about children's ability to identify syllables (mon/ster, stren/u/ous).

*Guided practice with prefixes and suffixes.* Write the same word several times on the board. Demonstrate how to add prefixes and suffixes. Children take turns writing prefixes and suffixes before and after the words. Assist children when necessary. Read the words together in chorus before going on to the next activity.

*Identify meaning families.* Have children find words with the Greek and Latin roots they are learning. Look in the dictionary, in your classroom, in books, and in the community. Children write the words they find on a chart and underline the root. Have a small group organize the found words into meaning families.

## Informal Assessment in the Classroom

*Checklists.* Take stock of the prefixes and suffixes you expect children to learn. Figure 3–15 is a list of prefixes, suffixes, and Greek and Latin roots that are frequently included in classroom reading programs. Use this list to assist you in determining which word parts children know and which parts they need to learn. Compare it with your classroom reading program. Add or delete items as appropriate.

**Figure 3–15**
Checklist for Common Prefixes, Suffixes, and Greek and Latin Roots

**COMMON PREFIXES**

| | | |
|---|---|---|
| _____ anti- | _____ com- | _____ dis- |
| _____ ex- | _____ il, in, im, ir meaning not | |
| _____ inter- | _____ mid- | _____ mis- |
| _____ non- | _____ out- | _____ over- |
| _____ post- | _____ pre- | _____ re- |
| _____ semi- | _____ sub- | _____ super- |
| _____ trans- | _____ un- | |

**COMMON SUFFIXES**

| | | |
|---|---|---|
| _____ -able | _____ -age | _____ -ance/ence |
| _____ -ave | _____ -ent | _____ -er |
| _____ -ful | _____ -fully | _____ -hood |
| _____ -ism | _____ -ish | _____ -ity/ty |
| _____ -ive | _____ -less | _____ -ment |
| _____ -ness | _____ -or | _____ -ous |
| _____ -ship | _____ -tion/sion/ion | |
| _____ -ture | _____ -wise | |

**COMMON GREEK AND LATIN ROOTS**

| | |
|---|---|
| _____ aster (star) | _____ aud (hear) |
| _____ bi (two) | _____ chronos (time) |
| _____ crat (rule) | _____ dec (ten) |
| _____ dic (speak) | _____ duc(t) (lead) |
| _____ fin (end) | _____ firm (strong) |
| _____ graph (write) | _____ hydro (water) |
| _____ ject (throw) | _____ logy (study of) |
| _____ magn (great) | _____ meter (measure) |
| _____ micro (small) | _____ multi (many) |
| _____ oct (eight) | _____ phon (sound) |
| _____ port (carry) | _____ rupt (break) |
| _____ scop (see) | _____ spec (look) |
| _____ sphere (ball) | _____ tele (far) |
| _____ therm (heat) | _____ tri (three) |
| _____ uni (one) | _____ vis (see) |

*Prefixes and suffixes.* Figure 3–16 is an informal assessment of the child's ability to read words with inflected endings. Children should read these words quickly and accurately well before the end of second grade. The Use Your Fingers strategy is a good tool to develop the ability to find prefixes and suffixes added to familiar words.

**Figure 3–16**
Informal
Assessment
Words with
Inflected Endings

---

*-s(-es),   -ed,   -ing,   -er,   -est,   -ly*

Select words from the material children are reading or use the list below. Ask the child to read the words. Words should be read correctly on the first try. Words the child reads instantly are known; words the child hesitates or sounds out are partially known; words the child guesses are not known.

Put a ✓ for instantly recognized words; draw a line for words the child self-corrects or sounds out (—); put a 0 for words the child guesses or does not read.

| | | | |
|---|---|---|---|
| plays | _____ | nicely | _____ |
| looked | _____ | bigger | _____ |
| jumping | _____ | sweeter | _____ |
| carried | _____ | bubbly | _____ |
| hopping | _____ | sadly | _____ |
| cries | _____ | maddest | _____ |
| baked | _____ | prettier | _____ |
| sitting | _____ | shortest | _____ |
| tried | _____ | slowly | _____ |
| flies | _____ | happiest | _____ |

The child reads these words.

| | |
|---|---|
| plays | nicely |
| looked | bigger |
| jumping | sweeter |
| babied | bubbly |
| hopping | sadly |
| cries | maddest |
| baked | prettier |
| sitting | shortest |
| tried | slowly |
| flies | happiest |

*Spelling words with inflected endings.* Adding inflected endings to common words can be difficult for some children. Conventions like doubling the last consonant (*hopped*) or adding *-es* to words ending in *s, ss, ch, sh, x,* or *z* are worth assessing. Use the informal spelling assessment in Figure 3–17 to determine the child's ability to spell words with common suffixes. Figure 3–17 also explains the eight conventions for spelling words with inflected endings.

**Figure 3–17**
Informal
Assessment
Spelling Words
with Inflected
Endings

---

**GENERALIZATIONS FOR ADDING SUFFIXES**

1. Add *-s* and *-ly* to one-syllable words with the CVC short vowel pattern (*hops*).
2. Double the last consonant before adding *-ed, -ing,* and *-er* to words ending with the CVC short vowel pattern (*hopped*).
3. Simply add *-s, -ed, -ing, -ly,* and *-er* to words ending in a CVCC short vowel pattern (*rested*).
4. Drop the final *e* and then add the *-ed, -ing,* or *-er* to words ending in a silent VCe (*baking*).
5. Add *-s* and *-ly* to VCe long vowel words (*hopes,* timely).
6. When words end with a double vowel (VV) that represents the long sound followed by a consonant, simply add *-s, -ed, -ing, -ly* and *-er* (cheaper).
7. Add *-s, -ed, -ing,* and *-er* to words ending in *ay, oy,* and *ey* (*toys*).
8. When a word ends in a *y,* change the *y* to an *i* before adding *-es, -ed* and *-er* (*dries*).

Ask the child to spell these words.

| -s, | -es, | -ies | -ed |
|---|---|---|---|
| *hops* | *buses* | *carries* | *hopped* |
| *rests* | *fishes* | *worries* | *rested* |
| *enjoys* | *benches* | | *dined* |
| *hopes* | *fixes* | | *carried* |
| *soaks* | *dries* | | *soaked* |
| *toys* | | | |

| -ing | -er | -est | -ly |
|---|---|---|---|
| *hopping* | *bigger* | *biggest* | *lowly* |
| *resting* | *softer* | *softest* | *softly* |
| *dining* | *nicer* | *nicest* | *nicely* |
| *carrying* | *sicker* | *sickest* | *sickly* |
| *soaking* | *cheaper* | *cheapest* | *cheaply* |
| *enjoying* | *worrier* | | |

*Contractions.* Use Activity 3.4, Undoing Contractions (Figure 3–4), to assess children's understanding of contractions. Ask children to undo the contractions you expect them to know and use, and make sure that individual children complete the activity without help from others. Use the information to determine the contractions that need to be reviewed.

*Syllables.* Here are two other classroom-friendly ways to informally assess the child's grasp of syllable patterns.

1. Ask the child to read 10 important complex words from the books the child is reading. Make sure the words are not already in the child's reading vocabulary. Asking the child to read familiar words will not give you a good idea of the child's ability to find syllables because familiar words are read by sight.

2. Ask the child to put slashes between syllables in a list of words you have copied from the text the child is reading. Analyze the slashes to determine the patterns the child (1) knows, (2) does not identify, or (3) confuses. Use the seven syllable patterns in this chapter to help you select words from the material children are reading.

## STRUCTURAL ANALYSIS IN THE CLASSROOM

### First and Second Grades

First and second graders learn to read and write compound words, contractions, a few high-utility prefixes such as *un-* and *re-* and often-used inflected endings like *-es/ies/s*, *-ed*, *-ing*, *-ly*, *-ful*, *-er*, *-est*, and *-ness*. Annalyse (Figure 3–18) is just beginning the second half of first grade. Notice that she uses suffixes (*annamols*). She recognizes some common suffixes, compound words, and most contractions. This makes it possible for Annalyse to identify and learn common words with often-used word parts. While Annalyse and other first and second graders learn some elements of word structure, phonics is the real focus. This will change in third grade when word structure figures more prominently in classroom reading programs.

**Figure 3–18**
Annalyse's Story

Annamols.
Annamols can be nacher and annamols can be trand you can bye them from the pet store and hope ther not a pain. Some annamols have spots and cm some annamols dont some annamols have strips and some dont. Annamols look difrint like me and you annamols dont look like enyyone not evan pooh.

*Continued on p. 84*

**Figure 3–18**
*Continued*

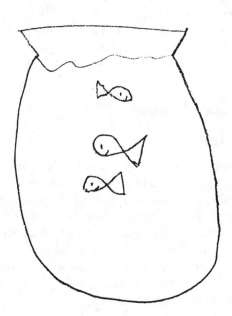

## WORKING WITH CHILDREN AT RISK

1. *Teach children to find word parts in complex words.* The reader at risk is apt to see a familiar word (*fill*) with a prefix or suffix (*refilled*) as a single unit and not notice its parts. The child then treats *refilled* as a new word rather than a known word (*fill*) with a prefix and suffix.

2. *Use caution when finding little words in big words.* This strategy is most likely to work with short words. It is not particularly helpful for complex words. We do not hear *dry* in *laundry*, *rat* in *literature*, or *plum* in *plumage*.

3. *Teach the most useful suffixes: -es/s, -ed, -ing, -ly, -er, and -or as in actor, -able and -ible, (t)ion.*

Children at risk are familiar with these suffixes in spoken language and, therefore, teaching them entails matching these familiar word parts with print (Champion, 1997).

4. *Develop dictionary skills.* Dictionary pronunciations are useful only when the struggling reader has some understanding of how to use the key. You will be a more effective teacher when you explicitly teach how the pronunciation key represents sound.

# Third, Fourth, Fifth, and Sixth Grades

Tamika (Figure 3–19) is a third grader; Joshua (Figure 3–20) is a fifth grader. Both children read and write complex words, and are developing a good working knowledge of less common prefixes and suffixes. Tamika is younger and, therefore, knows less about word structure than Joshua.

*Third grade.* Third grade is a bridge between the early grades (kindergarten, first, and second) and the upper grades (fourth, fifth, and sixth). Word structures—prefixes, suffixes, compound words, and contractions—taught in the early grades are revisited in

**Figure 3–19**
Tamika's Story

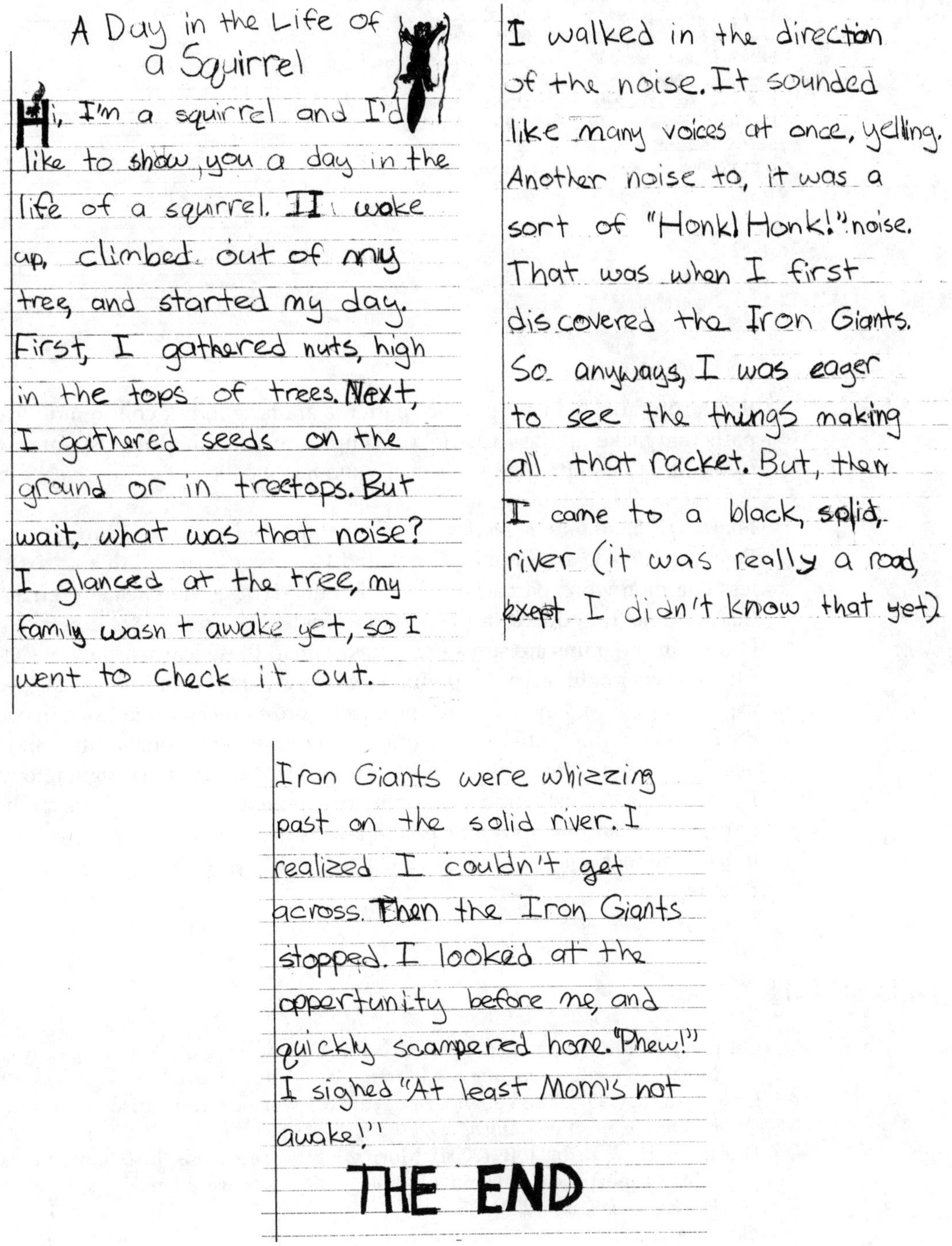

A Day in the Life of a Squirrel

Hi, I'm a squirrel and I'd like to show you a day in the life of a squirrel. I woke up, climbed out of my tree, and started my day. First, I gathered nuts, high in the tops of trees. Next, I gathered seeds on the ground or in treetops. But wait, what was that noise? I glanced at the tree, my family wasn't awake yet, so I went to check it out.

I walked in the direction of the noise. It sounded like many voices at once, yelling. Another noise to, it was a sort of "Honk! Honk!" noise. That was when I first discovered the Iron Giants. So anyways, I was eager to see the things making all that racket. But, then I came to a black, solid, river (it was really a road, exept I didn't know that yet)

Iron Giants were whizzing past on the solid river. I realized I couldn't get across. Then the Iron Giants stopped. I looked at the oppertunity before me, and quickly scampered home. "Phew!" I sighed "At least Mom's not awake!"

## THE END

**Figure 3–20**
Joshua's Story

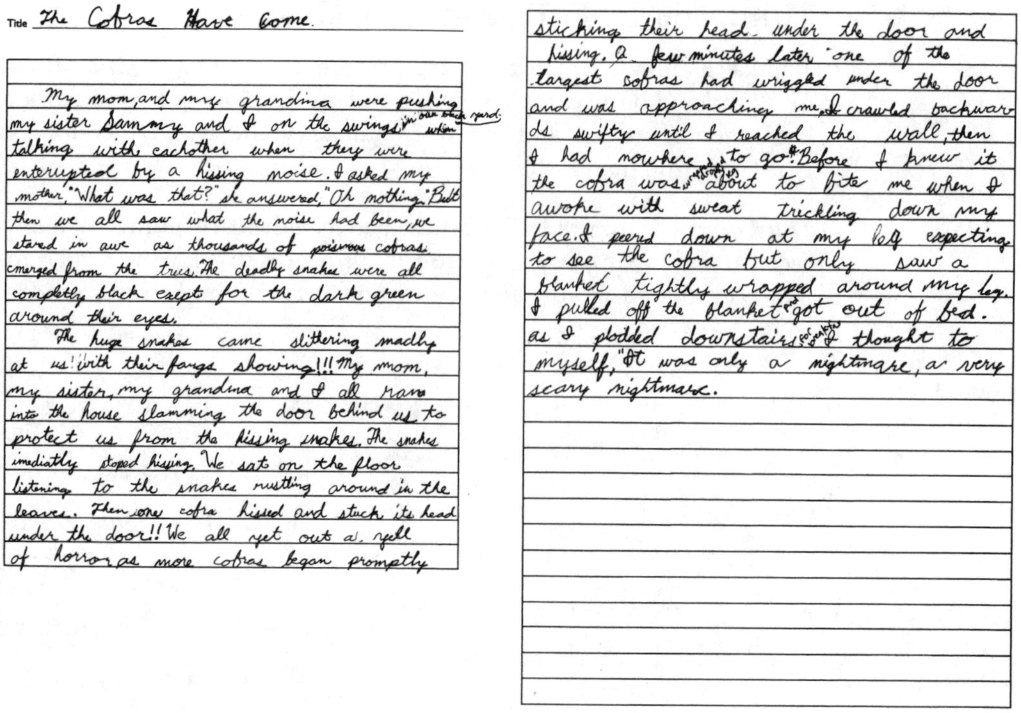

Title: The Cobras Have Come.

My mom, and my grandma were pushing my sister Sammy and I on the swings in our back yard, when talking with eachother when they were interrupted by a hissing noise. I asked my mother, "What was that?" she answered, "Oh nothing." But then we all saw what the noise had been, we stared in awe as thousands of poisonous cobras emerged from the trees. The deadly snakes were all completly black escept for the dark green around their eyes.

The huge snakes came slittering madly at us! with their fangs showing!!! My mom, my sister, my grandma and I all ran into the house slamming the door behind us to protect us from the hissing snakes. The snakes imediatly stoped hissing. We sat on the floor listening to the snakes rustling around in the leaves. Then one cobra hissed and stuck its head under the door!! We all yet out a yell of horror as more cobras began promptly

sticking their head under the door and hissing. A few minutes later one of the largest cobras had wriggled under the door and was approaching me. I crawled backwards swiftly until I reached the wall, then I had nowhere to go. Before I knew it the cobra was about to bite me when I awoke with sweat trickling down my face. I peered down at my leg expecting to see the cobra but only saw a blanket tightly wrapped around my leg. I pulled off the blanket got out of bed. as I plodded downstairs I thought to myself, "It was only a nightmare, a very scary nightmare.

the third grade. No new phonics patterns are taught, but children do learn new word parts that make up the structure of complex words. Children also infer word meaning from suffixes and prefixes such as *dis-* and *mis-*.

*Fourth, fifth, and sixth grades.* Word meaning and word structure are taught together. Fourth graders learn common Greek and Latin word parts; fifth and sixth graders learn less common word parts. Fourth, fifth, and sixth graders learn prefixes and suffixes that were not introduced in the previous grades. The prefixes and suffixes in fifth-grade classroom programs are somewhat trickier than those learned previously. For example, fifth graders might learn the prefixes *im-, ir-, il-,* and *in-* meaning "no," as in *impossible, irresponsible, illegal,* and *inactive.* The exact word parts children learn in each grade vary depending on the content and sequence of instruction. Fourth, fifth, and sixth graders learn Greek and Latin roots and how to use these roots to gain insight into word meaning. By the end of the sixth grade, children are expected to know and use all the syllable patterns, understand how syllable accent affects the pronunciation of words, identify base (*barely*) and root (*aquarium*) words, and use Greek and Latin roots to gain insight into word meaning.

# REFERENCES

Carlisle, J. F. (2000). Awareness of the structure and meaning of morphologically complex words: Impact on reading. *Reading and Writing: An Interdisciplinary Journal, 12,* 169–190.

Champion, A. (1997). The knowledge of suffixed words: A comparison of reading disabled and nondisabled readers. *Annals of Dyslexia, 47,* 29–55.

Deacon, S. H., & Kirby, J. R. (2004). Morphological awareness: Just "more phonological"? The roles of morphological and phonological awareness in reading development. *Applied Psycholinguistics, 25,* 223–238.

Eldredge, J. L. (2005). Foundations of fluency: An exploration. *Reading Psychology, 26,* 161–181.

Leong, C. K. (2000). Rapid processing of base and derived forms of words and grades 4, 5 and 6 children's spelling. *Reading and Writing: An Interdisciplinary Journal, 12,* 277–302.

Manzo, A. V., Manzo U. C., & Thomas, M. T. (2006). Rationale for systematic vocabulary development: Antidote for state mandates. *Journal of Adolescent & Adult Literacy, 49,* 610–619.

Nagy, W.,. Berninger, V. W., & Abbott, R. D. (2006). Contributions of morphology beyond phonology to literacy outcomes of upper elementary and middle-school students. *Journal of Educational Psychology, 98,* 134–147.

Pérez Cañado, M. L. (2005). English and Spanish spelling: Are they really different? *The Reading Teacher, 58,* 522–530.

White, T. G., Sowell, J., & Yanagihara, A. (1989). Teaching elementary students to use word part clues. *The Reading Teacher, 42,* 302–308.

**Answer:** The 28 variations of *use* are joined by *ill-use, misuse, reusing,* and *usability* for 32 words. Did you think of words that are not on the list?

# 4
# MEANING VOCABULARY

Imagine that you are waiting in a long, slow line at the checkout counter of your neighborhood grocery store. You notice magazines and weekly publications nestled among the candy bars, gum, and mints. Suddenly you start reading the captions and headlines on the magazines even though you had no intention of doing so. The publishers of those startling headlines and evocative article titles count on your inclination to instantly recognize words and understand messages in your environment. You use word meaning and life experiences to understand the titles and infer the general subject of articles. Publishers are hoping, of course, to use the startling titles to prompt you to purchase their publications.

## VOCABULARY MAKES FLUENT
## READING AND COMPREHENSION POSSIBLE

Sarah (Figure 4–1) recognizes and understands the meaning of almost all the words in text. She reads with better comprehension and greater fluency than her classmates who recognize and understand fewer words. A large reading vocabulary makes it possible for Sarah to read with expression and good phrasing and to concentrate on comprehension (August, 2006; Eldredge, 2005; Kame'enui & Bauman, 2004; Roberts & Neal, 2004).

**Figure 4–1**
Sharing Reaction

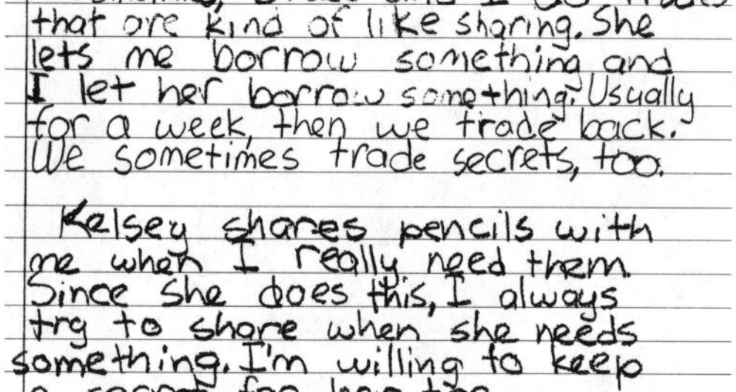

> Sometimes, Grace and I do trades that are kind of like sharing. She lets me borrow something and I let her borrow something. Usually for a week, then we trade back. We sometimes trade secrets, too.
>
> Kelsey shares pencils with me when I really need them. Since she does this, I always try to share when she needs something. I'm willing to keep a secret for her, too.

A large reading vocabulary frees the mind to think about meaning (explained in the Introduction). Freeing the mind is important because attention is limited. Readers either concentrate on figuring out words or think about meaning, but they cannot do both at once. The more attention that goes into figuring out the identity of words, the less attention the reader is able to direct to comprehension. If the text has too many unfamiliar words, readers divert so much attention away from comprehension that they cannot make sense of what they read.

The relationship between vocabulary and comprehension is reciprocal. As the child's vocabulary grows so the child's ability to understand text also improves (Martin-Chang & Levy, 2005). In the other direction, as the child's comprehension improves the child reads more difficult text. More difficult text introduces new words. The more new words the child encounters, the greater the likelihood that these words will be added to the child's reading vocabulary.

# THE WORDS THAT MATTER THE MOST

Reading vocabulary consists of all the words children instantly recognize and understand. Some words occur quite often. Of the 1,000 most frequently used words for beginning readers, a mere 300 account for a whopping 65% of the words in text. Children learn to automatically recognize often-used words because they read and write these words time and again (Beck, McKeown, & Kucan, 2002). You do not need to teach the meaning of these words because children already use them in everyday conversations.

Rare words are a second type of word. Rare words occur so infrequently that they have little likelihood of affecting comprehension and hence it is not worthwhile spending precious class time to teach these words (Beck, McKeown, & Kucan, 2002). The third group consists of words that occur occasionally (Beck, McKeown, & Kucan, 2002). It is important to teach these words because (1) they are important for comprehension and (2) children may not see or hear them often enough to learn them on their own. For example, the reader is far more likely to come across *baby* than *toddler* or *infant*. Although readers come across *infant* and *toddler* only occasionally, these words appear with enough regularity to make them useful for readers to understand.

For the purposes of organizing classroom instruction, we will divide words into six categories: (1) multiple-meaning words, (2) homophones (words that sound alike but differ in spelling, such as *sail–sale*), (3) synonyms (words with nearly the same meaning), (4) antonyms (words with the opposite meaning), (5) special words in content subjects, such as *decimal* and *subtract*, and (6) the special words children want to know.

## Multiple-Meaning Words

Many words have more than one meaning. For example, *band* refers to a group of musicians in "He played in the band" and to a ring in "She wore a gold wedding band." Readers use context clues to help them figure out which meaning is appropriate. Text for fourth, fifth, and sixth graders uses more multiple-meaning words than the text read by children in lower grades. Table 4–1 is a list of common multiple-meaning words that are important for understanding text.

## Homophones

Homophones sound alike but differ in spelling (*sail–sale* or *site–sight*). Children are far more likely to misspell homophones than to mispronounce them. Teach the simpler homophones in first and second grade, such as *sail–sale.* In third through sixth grade, single out for special attention the homophones children routinely confuse when writing, such as *there–their–they're*, or homophones with meanings that are difficult to differentiate, such as *principal–principle.* Table 4–2 is a list of homophones for reading and writing.

**TABLE 4–1  Multiple-Meaning Words**

| | | | | |
|---|---|---|---|---|
| act | face | hit | panel | sign |
| back | fair | hold | park | slip |
| bail | fall | horn | part | snap |
| band | fan | jam | pass | sound |
| bar | figure | jar | pit | space |
| bat | finish | land | play | spade |
| bill | flock | lead | point | stamp |
| block | foot | leak | position | stand |
| box | foul | leave | press | star |
| burst | frame | level | print | step |
| can | free | light | ram | stock |
| check | gear | line | rest | strain |
| chip | good | load | right | suit |
| coat | grade | low | ring | take |
| cool | hail | make | root | tax |
| court | hand | mark | round | thread |
| crane | handle | mean | run | toast |
| culture | harbor | mine | saw | track |
| current | hard | open | seal | train |
| deck | head | order | sharp | treat |
| degree | heel | organ | shell | watch |
| diamond | high | outline | show | wave |
| well | will | | | |

## Synonyms and Antonyms

Synonyms are words that have nearly the same meaning. *Beautiful* is a synonym for *pretty*; *famished* and *ravenous* are synonyms for *hungry*. Antonyms have the opposite meaning. *Sad* is an antonym for *happy*; *small* an antonym for *large*; *full* is the opposite of *empty*. A good working knowledge of synonyms and antonyms supports comprehension and helps children write more interesting text.

---

### BEST PRACTICES FOR EFFECTIVE TEACHING

1. *Preteach words that are necessary for comprehension* (National Reading Panel, 2000). Preteaching the meaning of important words improves comprehension and results in better fluency (Burns, Dean, & Foley, 2004).

2. *Make sure children read the same words repeatedly in different books.* Vocabulary increases when children read the same words often (Kamil, 2004).

3. *Use words children already understand when you clarify the meaning of new words.* Using familiar words makes it possible for children to connect the meaning of new words to their own experiences, concepts, and current meaning vocabulary.

4. *Teach words throughout the day and through content-area instruction.* Developing an understanding of words as children read and learn about content subjects facilitates comprehension and understanding word meaning.

5. *Develop breadth and depth of vocabulary.* Breadth is the size of children's vocabulary; depth is how much the child knows about words. It is important for children to know many words, but it is also important for children to know shades of meaning and how words relate to each other.

## TABLE 4-2 Homophones for Reading and Writing

| | | | | | |
|---|---|---|---|---|---|
| add | ad | compliment | complement | in | inn |
| aid | aide | coral | choral | insight | incite |
| air | heir, err | cord | chord | its | it's |
| aisle | isle, I'll | core | corps | kernel | colonel |
| allowed | aloud | council | counsel | knew | new, gnu |
| alter | altar | course | coarse | lair | layer |
| an | Ann | creek | creak | leak | leek |
| ant | aunt | cruel | crewel | lean | lien |
| ark | arc | cue | queue | least | leased |
| ate | eight | current | currant | led | lead |
| ax | acts | days | daze | lesson | lessen |
| bail | bale | dear | deer | lie | lye |
| ball | bawl | die | dye | links | lynx |
| band | banned | do | dew, due | loan | lone |
| baron | barren | doe | dough | loot | lute |
| base | bass | duel | dual | made | maid |
| based | baste | earn | urn | mail | male |
| basis | bases | ewe | yew | mall | maul |
| bazaar | bizarre | facts | fax | main | mane |
| be | bee | faint | feint | manner | manor |
| beach | beech | fair | fare | marry | merry, Mary |
| bear | bare | fairy | ferry | maze | maize |
| beat | beet | feet | feat | meet | meat, mete |
| bell | belle | foul | fowl | metal | mettle, medal |
| birth | berth | flare | flair | might | mite |
| bite | byte | flea | flee | miner | minor |
| blue | blew | flew | flue | moat | mote |
| board | bored | flower | flour | moose | mousse |
| bore | boar | four | for, fore | more | moor |
| boulder | bolder | fourth | forth | morn | mourn |
| bow | beau | freeze | frieze | morning | mourning |
| bow | bough | fur | fir | muscle | mussel |
| bowl | boll | gate | gait | naval | navel |
| brake | break | grease | Greece | need | kneed |
| bread | bred | great | grate | new | knew |
| bridle | bridal | grown | groan | night | knight |
| broach | brooch | guilt | gilt | no | know |
| brows | browse | gym | Jim | none | nun |
| build | billed | hail | hale | nose | knows |
| burro | burrow | hair | hare | not | knot |
| bury | berry | hall | haul | oh | owe |
| by | bye, buy | have | halve | one | won |
| caller | collar | hay | hey | or | oar, ore |
| capital | capitol | heard | herd | our | hour |
| carrot | carat | heel | heal | ours | hours |
| cart | carte | he'll | heel | overdo | overdue |
| cash | cache | here | hear | owe | oh |
| cast | caste | hi | high | pail | pale |
| cause | caws | him | hymn | pain | pane |
| cereal | serial | hoard | horde | pair | pear, pare |
| cheap | cheep | hole | whole | past | passed |
| chili | chilly | horse | hoarse | patience | patients |

**TABLE 4–2** (*Continued*)

| | | | | | |
|---|---|---|---|---|---|
| choose | chews | hue | hew | pause | paws |
| claws | clause | I | eye | pedal | peddle, petal |
| close | clothes | idle | idol | peek | peak, pique |
| piece | peace | seize | seas, sees | thrown | throne |
| pier | peer | sell | cell | tide | tied |
| plane | plain | seller | cellar | tighten | titan |
| pole | poll | sense | cents | time | thyme |
| poor | pour, pore | senses | census | toad | towed |
| presence | presents | sent | cent, scent | toe | tow |
| prey | pray | shear | sheer | tray | trey |
| pride | pried | shoe | shoo | two | to, too |
| prince | prints | shoot | chute | vale | veil |
| principal | principle | shown | shone | vein | vane, vain |
| profit | prophet | side | sighed | vial | vile |
| purr | per | sight | site, cite | wade | weighed |
| quarts | quartz | sleigh | slay | wait | weight |
| rack | wrack | so | sew, sow | warn | worn |
| rain | reign, rein | sole | soul | waste | waist |
| raise | rays, raze | some | sum | way | weigh |
| read | reed | sore | soar | we | wee |
| red | read | stair | stare | we'd | weed |
| real | reel | stationary | stationery | week | weak |
| right | write, rite | steak | stake | we've | weave |
| ring | wring | steal | steel | whale | wail |
| road | rode | straight | strait | which | witch |
| roll | role | sun | son | whine | wine |
| rose | rows | surf | serf | who's | whose |
| rough | ruff | sweet | suite | wore | war |
| rung | wrung | sword | soared | would | wood |
| sacks | sax | tail | tale | wrap | rap |
| sail | sale | tea | tee | wrote | rote |
| sealing | ceiling | team | teem | wry | rye |
| see | sea | tear | tier | yolk | yoke |
| seed | cede | tense | tents | you | ewe |
| seem | seam | there | their, they're | you'll | yule |
| seen | scene | threw | through | you're | your |

## Special Words in Content Subjects

Every content subject has special words. For example, *perpendicular*, *photosynthesis*, and *chrysalis* have specific meanings in mathematics and biology. Words like these need to be directly, explicitly taught and incorporated into classroom reading, speaking, and writing experiences. The words that matter the most in content subjects are usually listed in the teacher's manual. Words are printed in boldface, placed in the margin, or defined in the glossary in children's textbooks.

## Special Words Children Want to Know

Every child wants to learn a few special words. Younger children are often interested in the holiday words and favorite foods, and the names of toys and television characters figure prominently in children's preferences in the early grades. As children begin to read chapter books, they may be intrigued by special characters and events in these books. Strange words fascinate third through fifth graders. These children are interested in the longest words in English; words with odd letter combinations; palindromes (words spelled the same forwards and backwards, such as *peep* and *pop*); tongue-tickling words found in rhyming poetry and jingles; and onomatopoeic words (words that resemble the sounds around us, such as "meow" for a cat's call and "tick tock" to approximate the sound of a clock ticking). (See pages 108–110, "Informal Assessment or Additional Practices for Observing and Developing Vocabulary.")

# ACTIVITIES

## 16 ACTIVITIES TO DEVELOP MEANING VOCABULARY

Whenever we teach word meaning we teach something about the content of the text through language. The most effective activities develop knowledge of word meaning through active engagement. These activities give the children in your classroom a chance to "try on" words, to see how words fit into the content they are studying and into their daily lives. Children understand the meaning of new words by connecting words with concepts and through experiences and interactions. Pair the activities in this chapter with ongoing reading and writing. Use words in teaching, in conversations, and in writing to and for children.

## 4.1    Talk Through

- Large group or small group
- Use to develop word meaning.

Talking around words connects new words with the child's prior knowledge (Piercey, 1982). Children's understanding of how new words fit into their lives makes for better learning and, not coincidentally, greater retention.

**Material:** Important words.

**Step-by-step directions:**

1. Write an important word on the board. Then write the word in a sentence and underline the word. For example, you might write *pollution*. Then you might write: Exhaust from automobiles causes <u>pollution</u>.

2. Ask questions that tie the word to children's past experience. For instance, you might ask: "Tom, you put your empty juice can in the recycle bin in the cafeteria. Why did you do that? George, what do you see coming out of the tailpipe of bus number 7? Who has seen litter on the street? Has anyone noticed smoke in the air? Where? When?"

3. After the children talk about their experiences, write *pollution* for the second time on the board. Divide *pollution* into the base word—*pollute*—and the suffix—*tion*: *pollute + tion*.

4. Explain word meaning and relate meaning to the children's experiences. "Pollution means harmful materials like exhaust fumes in the air. We can divide *pollution* into *pollute* and *tion*. *Pollute* means 'to make something impure,

like the exhaust from cars.' *Tion* means 'the state of.' So pollution is something harmful to our environment." Recall examples from the discussion. For instance, "Tamara, you noticed pollution in the air when you saw smoke. Maria, you saw pollution when you saw trash floating in the lake." and so forth.

## 4.2    Semantic Sorts with Coupons and Words

- Small group, pairs, individual, and learning center
- Use to develop word meaning.

Children first sort coupons into categories, followed by sorting words, and finally engage in a "grand" sort on the chalkboard. Sorting coupons is especially helpful for English learners and children who would benefit from additional opportunities to associate pictures with word meaning.

**Material:** Coupons children bring from home; a container to store all the coupons; as many smaller containers to hold coupons as there are sorting categories; cards with words for semantic sorting; 3- × 5-inch cards with words on one side and masking tape loops on the other for a group follow-up sort on the chalkboard (optional).

**Step-by-step directions:**

### Coupon Sorting

1. Have children bring coupons from home. Place the coupons in a small box until there are enough for children to sort.

2. Demonstrate how to sort coupons by semantic (meaning) category. Then place the large container and as many smaller containers as there are categories in a learning center. Individuals or pairs may sort coupons in the learning center.

3. Specify the categories for younger children. Label the containers with each category name. Easier sorts are targeted to specific types of items like (1) breakfast food, (2) pet food, and (3) chips and crackers. More challenging semantic sorts ask children to categorize according to larger, more superordinate groups, such as (1) food, (2) cleaning supplies, (3) paper products, and (4) personal care products.

4. Once children have sorted the coupons, remove them from the containers. Discuss the categories with the small group. Talk about the meaning of product names and the categories to which they might belong.

### Word Sorting

1. Distribute cards with words only. Have the group suggest categories for sorting, specify categories of your own (called closed sorts because the categories are specified), or allow children to determine their own categories (called open sorts because children create their own categories).

2. Place the cards in a learning center or divide a small group into pairs and have the pairs sort the words.

3. When the sorts are complete, ask children to tell about the words and the categories.

**Figure 4–2**
Semantic Sorts
with Coupons
and Words

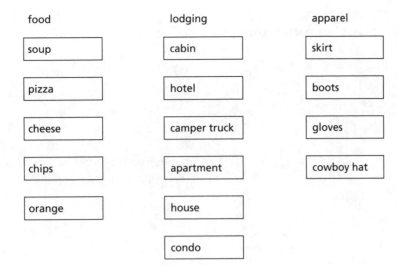

**Grand Chalkboard Sort**

1. Give each child one or more 5- × 8-inch cards with a word on one side and a masking tape loop on the other. The words may be the same as those the children have sorted previously (steps 1–3, above) or new words, depending on the children's development as readers.

2. Write categories on the board. Have children come to the board and place their words under the proper heading, as in Figure 4–2.

3. Talk about the way children sorted. Discuss words that could belong to more than one category (if appropriate).

## 4.3   Synonym Guessing

- Small group
- Use to develop knowledge of synonyms.

This fast-paced small-group guessing game helps children think of synonyms.

**Material:** Word cards.

**Step-by-step directions:**

1. Divide a small group into two teams. Ask one child from each team to sit in front of you. Team members sit behind the two players.

2. Hold up a word card. Do not show it to the two players.

3. The members on one team say a synonym and the child sitting in front of the teacher guesses the word. If the child does not guess the correct word, members of the opposite team give the child from their team a synonym clue.

4. The first player to identify the word earns one point for the team.

## 4.4    Antonym (or Synonym) Concentration

**Figure 4–3**
Antonym Concentration

| | | |
|---|---|---|
| gentle | | |
| | | |
| | harsh | |
| | | |
| success / failure | ill / healthy | |

- Pairs or learning center
- Use to develop knowledge of antonyms or synonyms.

In this version of concentration children remember the location of two face-down cards that show synonyms or antonyms.

**Material:** Pairs of cards with antonyms (*huge* and *small*) or synonyms (*huge* and *enormous*) children are learning.

**Step-by-step directions:**

1. Place the cards face down in rows. Children take turns turning up two cards.
2. When a child turns up antonyms (or synonyms), the child reads the words and keeps the cards (Figure 4–3).
3. The child with the most cards wins.

## 4.5    Acrostic Poems

- Small group, pairs, individual, or learning center
- Use to develop word meaning.

In acrostic poems a word is read vertically and the lines of the poem are read horizontally. Because each letter of the word begins a line of the poem, it is similar to a word puzzle and a good medium for describing concepts and complimenting individuals, as well as for exploring word meaning.

**Material:** Long words from the text children are reading; thesauruses; crayons, chalk, or colored markers (optional); construction paper (optional).

**Step-by-step directions:**

If children have not written acrostics before, write an acrostic with the whole class.

1. Children select a special word and write it letter-by-letter down the left side of the page.
2. Children think of sentences that describe the selected word. Each sentence begins with a letter in the selected word.

**Figure 4–4**
Acrostic Poem: Imagination

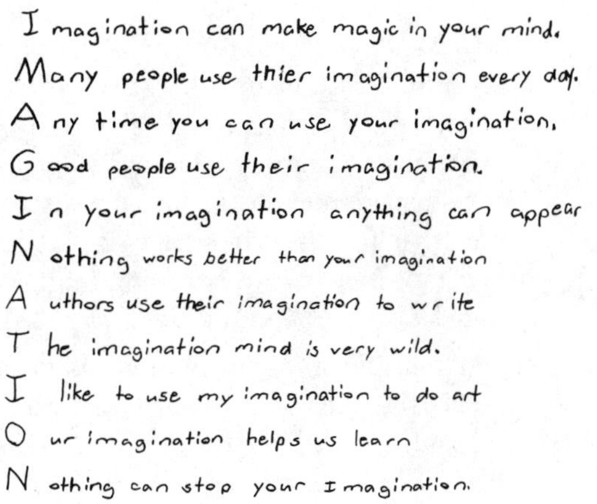

I magination can make magic in your mind.
Many people use thier imagination every day.
A ny time you can use your imagination.
G ood people use their imagination.
I n your imagination anything can appear
N othing works better than your imagination
A uthors use their imagination to write
T he imagination mind is very wild.
I like to use my imagination to do art
O ur imagination helps us learn
N othing can stop your Imagination.

**Figure 4–5**
Acrostic Poem: Transportation

T hen first railroad engine was called the "Tom Thumb."
R obert Fulton developed steam engines to power steam boats
A ir planes were made in 1903.
N ew types of transportation change the way people live.
S team boats were invented by Robert Fulton.
P eople use transportation all around the world.
O rville and Wilbur Wright made the first airplane.
R ocet ships are a type of transportation
T echnology was used to make transportation.
A melia Earhart disappeared in 1937 on a trip around the world.
T he Wright bro's made the first successful airplane flight.
I t is useful to use transportation.
O n the oregon trail people traveled by wagon train.
N ow and days, transportation is changed

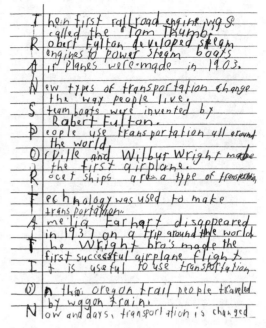

3. Write describing sentences horizontally, as we see in Figures 4–4 and 4–5.
4. Fourth and fifth graders benefit from using a thesaurus to find long words to replace overused words.
5. Acrostic poems are a good way to conclude a curriculum unit. Have children write an acrostic poem for a key word related to the curriculum unit. A child in a class finishing a unit on imagination wrote the acrostic poem in Figure 4–4. The poem in Figure 4–5 was written for the word *transportation,* which is a social studies unit of study.
6. Illustrate with a poster or drawing.

## 4.6 Concept Wheels

- Large group or small group
- Use to develop word meaning.

In making concept wheels children use background knowledge and their understanding of word meaning to name the concept that ties the ideas together (Rupley, Logan, & Nichols, 1999; Vacca et al., 2003).

**Material:** Nothing special.

**Step-by-step directions:**

1. Write a key concept word on the board.
2. Ask the group to brainstorm to think of everything they know about the word. Write ideas on the board.

## TEACHING ENGLISH LANGUAGE LEARNERS

1. *Develop concepts along with vocabulary.* Relate new concepts to the child's existing knowledge and introduce words through culturally relevant text (Feger, 2005).

2. *Read and reread books aloud in sections.* When we read books aloud in sections, not all at once, children focus on learning a few words at a time, which improves learning (Hickman, Pollard-Durodola, & Vaughn, 2004). Try singling out three or fewer words per section; read for comprehension first and then reread to call attention to vocabulary. Follow up with comprehension activities in which you and the children use the words in context.

3. *Teach cognates.* Cognates are words with similar sounds and meanings in two languages: *exit* and *éixto*. Cognates are a bridge to the child's home language. Because English and Spanish share many cognates, understanding cognates in these two languages is particularly important for Spanish-speaking English language learners (RAND Study Group, 2004).

4. *Make word meaning as obvious as possible.* Use all the senses to teach word meaning (Sadoski, 2005). Develop word knowledge with trips, films, software, murals, and dioramas. Draw pictures and use objects, drama, and facial gestures to help explain word meaning (Graves, Gersten, & Haager, 2004).

**Figure 4–6**
Concept Wheel for Camel

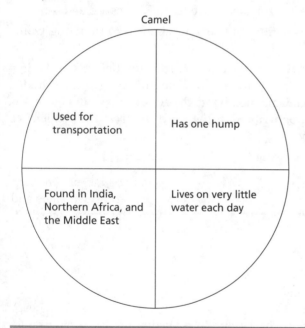

3. Draw a large circle; divide it into four sections.

4. Have a volunteer read the brainstormed ideas. Ask children to identify the four most important things about the subject.

5. Discuss and debate choices. Erase all but four key ideas. Write each one in a section, as we see in Figure 4–6.

6. Have groups of three children make concept wheels for key concept words in chapter books and content subjects. Display the wheels; ask groups to explain their wheels to their classmates.

## 4.7    Definition Bingo

- Small group
- Use to develop knowledge of word meaning.

In definition bingo children cover words that the teacher defines.

**Material:** Bingo cards with words children are learning; paper squares or chips.

**Figure 4–7**
Definition Bingo

| ponies | plume | dose | hike | sway |
|--------|-------|------|------|------|
| groan | soar | expert | gravity | patches |
| Scrub | lazy | FREE | clutch | orbit |
| position | summary | marsh | gobbler | loyal |
| thermos | labor | flatter | hutch | massive |

Definitions:
Select important words and definitions from the text children are reading. You may also want to select important words from the conversations and discussions in your classrom. Selecting words used in conversations is especially helpful for English language learners.

**Step-by-step directions:**

1. Distribute cards with the five columns divided into three rows with an X in the middle box, as shown in Figure 4–7.
2. Write a group of words on the board that children are learning. Write more words than bingo squares. Tell the children to use their best handwriting to write one word in each square. Ask children to mix up the words so that their card has words in squares different from their neighbor's card.
3. Distribute paper squares or tokens to cover the bingo words.
4. Randomly select a word; give a simple definition. Children listen for definitions and cover words you define.

## 4.8    Venn Diagrams

- Large or small group
- Use to develop word meaning.

Venn diagrams are two or three overlapping circles with shared characteristics in the overlapping portion and unique characteristics in the separate circles. These diagrams help children develop in-depth knowledge of how two objects or concepts are both similar and different. Venn diagrams are especially helpful in analyzing characters and settings in story text and developing a keen understanding of the special words in content-area subjects.

**Material:** Nothing special.

**Step-by-step directions:**

1. Select two important words. Discuss the words with the group.
2. Draw two overlapping circles as shown in Figure 4–8. Write a word in or above each circle.
3. Make a list of things children already know about word meanings. Discuss characteristics of the words' meanings and write them in the appropriate circle.
4. Now have children look in the story or informational text to find additional characteristics that are unique to each word. Write these characteristics in the circle.
5. Have children suggest shared characteristics. Write the shared characteristics in the overlapping portion. You might wish to have children find information in the story or informational text to support their suggestions.

**Figure 4–8**
Venn Diagram
for Passenger Liners
and Supertankers

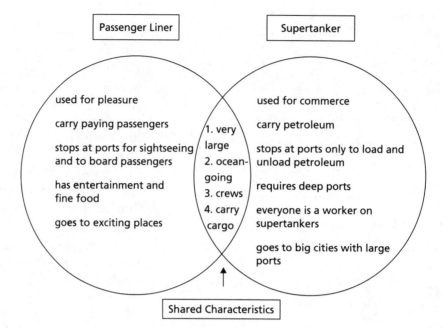

## 4.9   Definition Puzzles

- Large group, small group, pairs, individual, or learning center
- Use to develop word meaning.

Children use beginning letter and meaning clues to figure out the identity of missing words.

**Material:** Definition puzzles, as shown in Figure 4–9.

**Figure 4–9**
Definition Puzzle for
Words Children Are
Learning

1. not true                                              | f |   |   |   |   |   |   |

2. something handed down from generation to
   generation in a family                                | h |   |   |   |   |   |   |

3. very old                                              | a |   |   |   |   |   |   |

4. a person from whom you are descended                  | a |   |   |   |   |   |   |   |

5. a person belonging to the same family                 | r |   |   |   |   |   |   |   |

6. your mother's sister                                  | a |   |   |

7. your mother's brother                                 | u |   |   |   |

Answers: fiction, heirloom, ancient, ancestor, relative, aunt, uncle

**Step-by-step directions:**

1. Select important words related to a theme or content subject. Make as many boxes as letters in each word, and write the beginning letter in the first box. Write short definitions.
2. Children solve puzzles by thinking about the definition and word length.

## 4.10  Webs

- Large group, small group, or pairs
- Use to develop word meaning or for synonyms.

Use webs to explore the concepts associated with words in content subjects, the personalities of characters in books, or to expand children's vocabulary by thinking of alternatives for overused words (La Fromboise, 2000).

**Material:** Large pieces of paper; markers or pencils.

**Step-by-step directions:**

1. Discuss an important word.
2. Write the word in the center of a large piece of paper or on the board.
3. Write important meanings and characteristics around the word.
4. Draw lines to connect the center word with related words. Figure 4–10 is a synonym web for *big*.

Webs are effective when children talk about the words and are actively involved in constructing them.

**Figure 4–10**
Synonym Web for *Big*

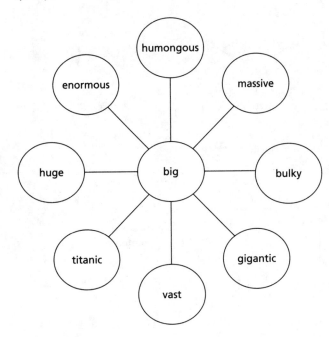

## 4.11  Vocabulary Concept Maps

- Large group, small group, or pairs
- Use to develop word meaning.

Concept maps are visual arrays that call for defining a new word in a variety of ways.

**Material:** One vocabulary concept map for each child in the group.

**Step-by-step directions:**

1. Select an important word from the text children are reading. Write the word on the board.
2. Discuss word meaning. Refer to the text for examples of word use.

3. Distribute the vocabulary concept maps. Children write the word in the center.

4. Have individuals or pairs define the word, use it in a sentence, provide examples and nonexamples, and draw a picture. Figures 4–11 and 4–12 are concept maps completed by a third grader.

5. Discuss the completed maps with the group. Invite children to share their maps.

**Figure 4–11**
Concept Map for *Vessel*

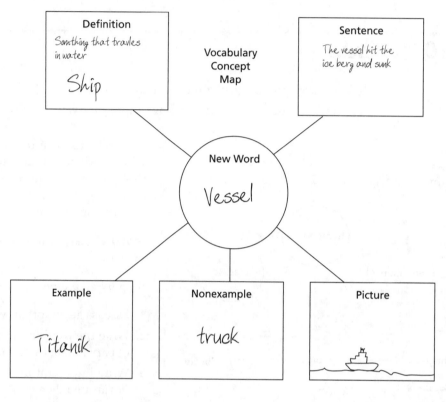

**Figure 4–12**
Concept Map for
*Scraggly*

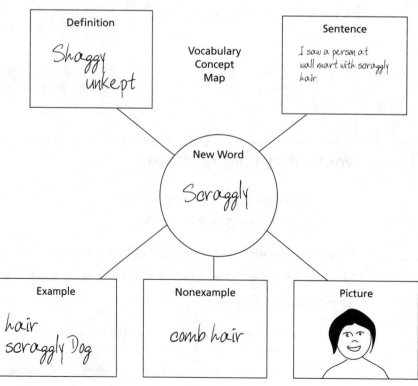

## 4.12    **Word Banks with Partners**

- Large group or small group
- Use to develop word meaning. Use with third, fourth, and fifth graders.

Word banks are small boxes in which children store the meanings of new words. In this twist to an old favorite, children make vocabulary cards with a word and definition on both sides and then take turns showing cards and talking about definitions with a partner (Piercey, 1982).

**Material:** A small box for each child; index cards to fit inside the box; tabs to show alphabetical order.

**Step-by-step directions:**

1. Have children make two-sided cards for key concept words and for words they would like to learn. Side 1 shows the underlined word in a sentence and a brief definition. Side 2 has the word underlined in a sentence.

2. Partners may make some word cards for the same key concept words. Other cards may be special cards one of the partners wants to learn.

3. Partners take turns showing each other the cards, reading the words, and discussing meaning. One child shows side 1 to the other child. The child looking at side 1 reads the sentence and defines the word. This gives the child practice seeing the words in a sentence and thinking of meaning. In Figure 4–13 the child would explain the meaning of *explosion*. The partner showing side 1 is

**Figure 4–13**
Word Banks with Partners

**SIDE 1**

One partner shows side 1 to the other partner.
The child showing side 1 sees the word, the sentence and the definition.

The other partner reads side 1 and gives the definition.
This gives both partners opportunities to associate meaning with the new word.

> explosion
>
> The <u>explosion</u> blew bricks and glass into the street.

**SIDE 2**

> explosion
>
> The <u>explosion</u> blew bricks and glass into the street.
>
> bursting or expanding suddenly and loudly

looking at side 2. Since side 2 has the word, the sentence, and the definition, this partner has an opportunity to learn word meaning while showing the word card to the partner.

4. Place the cards in alphabetical order in the box. Use the cards as a ready resource when writing, in games, and for informal assessment.

## 4.13    Association Circles

- Small group or pairs
- Use to develop word meaning.

Children select words from a familiar book and then create a word circle. In the circle each word is connected to the previous word and to the following word through its use in the story or in the content-subject textbook. In creating circles, children find, read, and write words; think about meaning; and relate meaning to story events or the information in textbooks.

**Material:** Paper and pencils; a storybook or content-subject textbook.

**Figure 4–14**
Association Circles

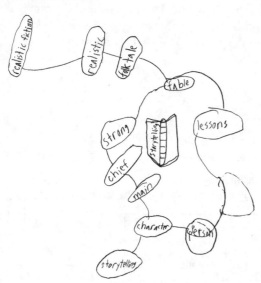

**Step-by-step directions:**

1. Demonstrate how to create a circle by inviting the group to suggest a pivotal word and words associated with it. Once children have created a circle as a whole group, ask them to create their own circles in pairs or individually.

2. Children first select a concept word from a content-area textbook or a key word from a current curriculum theme.

3. Pairs or individuals think of a word that is associated with the target word and then use the second word to trigger a third word, and so on.

4. Connect words one-by-one, with each word having a meaningful relationship with its immediate predecessor. The circle in Figure 4–14 expresses the connections made among words, events, and ideas in a story about a legend.

## 4.14    Homophone Spelling and Puzzles

- Pairs, individual or learning center
- Use to develop knowledge of homophones.

Spelling and solving puzzles help children discover the spelling and meaning of homophones.

**Homophone Spelling**
**Material:** Nothing special.

**Figure 4–15**
Homophone
Puzzles

| | | |
|---|---|---|
| 1. | Something we eat | m_____ |
| 2. | Introduced to | m_____ |

meet–meat

| | | |
|---|---|---|
| 1. | A large body of water | s_____ |
| 2. | To look | s_____ |

sea–see

| | | |
|---|---|---|
| 1. | Form letters or words | w_____ |
| 2. | Correct | w_____ |

write–right

| | | |
|---|---|---|
| 1. | A fruit | p_____ |
| 2. | Two that belong together | p_____ |

pear–pair

| | | |
|---|---|---|
| 1. | A number | e_____ |
| 2. | Have eaten | a_____ |

eight–ate

| | | |
|---|---|---|
| 1. | It grows in the garden. | f_____ |
| 2. | It is used in bread and cake. | f_____ |

flower–flour

| | | |
|---|---|---|
| 1. | You can buy it for a cheaper price | s_____ |
| 2. | It is necessary for some boats to move. | s_____ |

sale–sail

| | | |
|---|---|---|
| 1. | It falls from the sky. | r_____ |
| 2. | Riders use it to guide a horse. | r_____ |
| 3. | Something kings and queens do. | R_____ |

rain–rein–reign

| | | |
|---|---|---|
| 1. | Something on your foot. | t_____ |
| 2. | To pull something | t_____ |

toe–tow

**Step-by-step directions:**

1.  Identify from five to ten homophone pairs. Dictate one homophone from each pair.
2.  Children write the words you dictate.
3.  When finished, write the homophones you dictated on the board. Ask children to work in groups of two or three to compare the words they wrote with the words you dictated (and later wrote on the board).
4.  Discuss how two words sound alike but look different. Also talk about word meaning.

**Homophone Puzzles**

**Material:** Homophones; a crossword puzzle for the homophones. Write a list of homophones with short definitions, as shown in Figure 4–15.

**Step-by-step directions:**

1.  Children work individually or in pairs to complete puzzles.
2.  Follow-up by having children make their own puzzles and then sharing the puzzles with others in your class.

---

## 4.15  Sensory Images in Poetry

- Large group, small group, or pairs
- Use to develop word meaning.

Children select words from poems that bring sensory images to mind. Use this activity for group discussion or as a follow-up after reading poetry.

**Material:** Poems; sensory catalog, as shown in Figure 4–16.

**Step-by-step directions:**

1.  Read and discuss one or more poems with the group.
2.  Give each individual or pair a sheet similar to the one shown in Figure 4–16. Children write words that evoke one or more of the five senses (sight, sound, smell, taste, touch).

**Figure 4–16**
Sensory Images in Poetry

**SENSORY CATALOG**

Poem_____

Words that remind me of how things look, how they sound, how they might taste, how they smell and how they feel.

| Sight | Sound | Taste | Smell | Touch |
|-------|-------|-------|-------|-------|
| _____ | _____ | _____ | _____ | _____ |
| _____ | _____ | _____ | _____ | _____ |
| _____ | _____ | _____ | _____ | _____ |
| _____ | _____ | _____ | _____ | _____ |

# 4.16    Semantic Networks

Semantic networks (1) help the child develop insight into the interconnectedness of concepts and ideas and (2) create graphic displays that show how concepts are related (Stahl & Nagy, 2005).

**Material:** A chalk- or whiteboard; pencils and paper for pairs or small groups.

**Step-by-step directions:**

**Before reading**

1. Write a word that labels an important concept and draw a circle around it.
2. Children brainstorm to think of everything they know about the concept. You write the words on the board.

**During reading**

3. Children read the text and write down other words that describe or are related to the concept.

**After reading**

4. Add the words children wrote during reading to the words on the board.
5. The group discusses which words, ideas, and examples are relevant to the concept. Erase words, ideas, and examples that the group judges to be too far afield from the concept.
6. Have the group suggest ways to arrange the words. Draw bubbles around each and connect them with lines, as shown in Figure 4–17.

**Figure 4–17**
Semantic Network
for *Water*

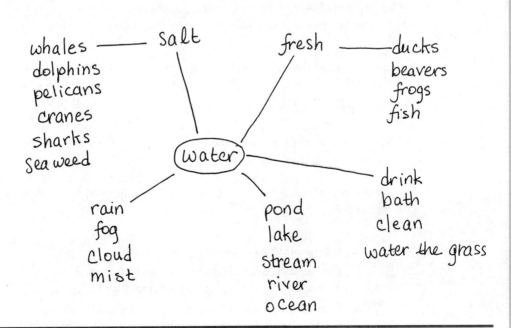

# INFORMAL ASSESSMENT OR ADDITIONAL PRACTICES FOR OBSERVING AND DEVELOPING VOCABULARY

## Additional Practices

*Context clues.* Context clues can help the reader understand word meaning when (1) the reader knows all the words in the sentence except the new word, (2) the surrounding words clarify the meaning of a new word, and (3) the reader is able to infer word meaning from the context clues (Fukkink, 2005; McKeown & Beck, 2004). Make children aware of these context clues to word meaning:

1. *Definition.* Look for *is* and *called* in sentences like "Knights carried a long spear *called* a lance."

2. *Examples.* Words like *such as*, *for example*, and *like* indicate an example. "Grandma loved shellfish *like* clams and lobsters."

3. *Restatements.* Pay attention to *that is, in other words, or,* and *put another way.* "Our baseball team is going to the semifinals. *In other words*, we will compete in the last game before the final matchup."

4. *Synonyms.* Show children how to relate a new word to a known word by substituting a familiar word for the new word in a sentence like "Officer Smith used a trained canine to find the lost children." Tell children to read the whole sentence, then reread it again substituting the familiar word *dog* for *canine* ("Officer Smith used a trained dog to find the lost children"), and reread the sentence a third time with the new word in its proper place ("Officer Smith used a trained canine to find the lost children").

5. *Antonyms.* Help children become sensitive to words with opposite or different meanings, as in the sentence "The *buoyant* stick floated on the water while the *heavy* stone sank to the bottom of the pond."

*Rereading read-aloud books.* Read and discuss a new word during each reading. Rereading the same book and talking about a new word during each rereading significantly increases children's understanding of word meaning (Biemiller & Boote, 2006; Coyne, Simmons, Kame'enui, & Stoolmiller, 2004).

*Clues to word meaning in information text.* Teach children to use the features of information text—bold words, words in margins, words defined in chapters, or the glossary—to learn word meaning.

*The dictionary.* Dictionaries support reading by clarifying the meaning of a word when context clues are too weak for the reader to infer meaning. Although the dictionary is a tool for finding the correct spelling, children use word processor spelling checks and handheld devices more often. Try these suggestions for effective dictionary instruction:

1. Teach children how to use guide words.

2. Help children become familiar with dictionaries by asking them to look up words they already know something about (Stahl & Nagy, 2006).

3. Show children how to use the dictionary while reading. Children are more likely to value the dictionary as a word learning tool when they use it while reading.

## Informal Assessment in the Classroom

Listening to children talk about stories, discuss poetry, and explain content subject ideas gives us an idea of children's grasp of word meaning. Questions give us a little more information about what the child thinks and the depth of the child's word knowledge. Try asking questions like:

1. Do you see any hard words in this story/text? What are they? What do they mean?
2. What does _____ mean in this sentence?
3. Can you think of another meaning (or another word) for _____?
4. What is the opposite of _____?
5. What do I mean when I say _____?
   **(The flower drank up the sun's ray.)**
6. Use _____ in a sentence.

*Maze sentences.* The maze technique assesses vocabulary in context, as well as the child's ability to recognize words. To construct maze sentences, select sentences from the books children are reading. Delete a key concept word in each sentence. Replace the word with a blank and two choices. The child uses word knowledge and context to select the correct word.

*Mexico is a _____ to the south of the United States.*
   **county, country**

*KWL charts.* KWL charts guide children in applying prior knowledge to reading, setting purposes, and verifying information (Ogle, 1986). KWL charts consist of three columns. Children write what they know about a key concept in the "K" column. Analyzing this column gives you insight into the words the child needs to learn more about.

*Self-assessment.* Select key concept words from the material children are reading. Use the word knowledge assessment in Figure 4–18 to get an idea of children's knowledge

**Figure 4–18**
Self-Assessment
of Word
Knowledge

| Name_____ | | |
|---|---|---|
| | **Some things I know about this word.** | **I don't know this word.** |
| **earthquake** | **when the ground shakes** | |
| **chasm** | | ✓ |
| | | |
| | | |

of key words. This self-assessment is particularly useful for assessing children's knowledge of words they need to know in order to understand text. Give children a short list of words. Have them put a ✓ by words they do not know. Multiple-meaning words are problematic for this type of self-assessment because children may know a meaning that does not correspond to the meaning you are teaching.

## VOCABULARY IN THE CLASSROOM

### Kindergarten, First, and Second Grades

Kindergartners and first graders learn to classify and sort pictures that represent familiar words and learn to describe familiar objects and events. First graders also learn common compound words. Second graders explain simple synonyms and antonyms, read simple compound words, and use context and the dictionary to clarify word meaning. Kindergarten through second-grade teachers read aloud often and discuss word meaning, demonstrate and illustrate meaning, engage all the senses in helping children learn word meaning, and develop the background experiences necessary for children to learn new words. Teachers do these things to a greater or lesser extent depending on children's understanding of the words in text.

### WORKING WITH CHILDREN AT RISK

1. *Develop vocabulary through direct instruction and experiences reading and writing.* Direct instruction and incidental learning are important and both should have a prominent place in your classroom reading program (Rupley & Nichols, 2005).

2. *Spend extra time developing reading vocabulary.* Generally speaking, it takes more direct instruction to teach new words to at-risk children than to average readers (Cain, Oakill, & Lemmon, 2004).

3. *Guide children toward relatively easy books for leisure reading.* Children are more likely to learn new words when they read books with few new words than when they read books that have many unfamiliar words and concepts.

4. *Emphasize context clues when the clues are near new words in text.* Encourage children to use the reading context when information about word meaning is next to or near the new word in text (Cain, Oakhill, & Elbro, 2003). Directly teach the meaning of words when context clues are not adjacent to new words.

5. *Teach vocabulary in context.* Teaching vocabulary in context results in better memory for words, greater use of words in conversation, and better comprehension than teaching definitions (Nash & Snowling, 2006).

### Third, Fourth, Fifth, and Sixth Grades

Children continue to learn how prefixes and suffixes affect word meaning. Classroom programs include teaching children to use the features of information text to learn word meaning. Third graders use the reading context and knowledge of antonyms, synonyms, multiple-meaning words, and homophones to uncover word meaning. Children may also learn to categorize words based on superordinate categories—energy sources consist of the sun, gasoline, wood, wind, water, for example. Fourth through sixth graders use meaningful word parts (explained in chapter 3) and the reading context to infer meaning. Fifth graders learn to explain figurative expressions and to use a thesaurus. By sixth grade, children learn the meaning of similes and metaphors as well as the different shades of meaning associated with multiple-meaning words. By the time sixth graders graduate to seventh grade, they are learning words much as mature readers.

# REFERENCES

August, D. (2006). *Developing literacy in second-language learners: Report of the national literacy panel on language-minority children and youth, executive summary.* Retrieved April 14, 2006, from http://www.cal.org/natl-lit-panel/reports/Executive_Summary.pdf

Beck, I. L., McKeown, M. G., & Kucan, L. (2002). *Bringing words to life: Robust vocabulary instruction.* New York: Guilford Press.

Biemiller, A., & Boote, C. (2006). An effective model for building meaning vocabulary in primary grades. *Journal of Educational Psychology, 98,* 44–62.

Burns, M. K., Dean, V. J., & Foley, S. (2004). Preteaching unknown key words with incremental rehearsal to improve reading fluency and comprehension with children identified as reading disabled. *Journal of School Psychology, 42,* 303–314.

Cain, K., Oakhill, J. V., & Elbro, C. (2003). The ability to learn new word meanings with and without context by school-age children with and without language comprehension difficulties. *Journal of Child Language, 30,* 681–694.

Cain, K., Oakhill, J. V., & Lemmon, K. (2004). Individual differences in the inference of word meanings from context: The influence of reading comprehension, vocabulary knowledge, and memory capacity. *Journal of Educational Psychology, 96,* 671–681.

Coyne, M. D., Simmons, D. C., Kame'enui, E. J., & Stoolmiller, M. (2004). Teaching vocabulary during shared storybook reading: An examination of different effects. *Exceptionality, 12,* 145–162.

Eldredge, J. L. (2005). Foundations of fluency: An exploration. *Reading Psychology, 26,* 161–181.

Feger, M. V. (2005). "I want to read": How culturally relevant texts increase students engagement in reading. *Multicultural Education, 13,* 18–19.

Fukkink, R. G. (2005). Deriving word meaning from written context: A process analysis. *Learning and Instruction, 15,* 23–43.

Graves, A. W., Gersten, R., & Haager, D. (2004). Literacy instruction in multiple-language first-grade classrooms: Linking student outcomes to observed instructional practice. *Learning Disabilities Research & Practice, 19,* 262–272.

Hickman, P., Pollard-Durodola, S., & Vaughn, S. (2004). Storybook reading: Improving vocabulary and comprehension for English-language learners. *The Reading Teacher, 57,* 720–730.

Kame'enui, E. J., & Bauman, J. F. (2004). Vocabulary: The plot of the reading story. In J. F. Bauman & E. J. Kame'enui (Eds.), *Vocabulary instruction: Research to practice* (pp. 3–10). New York: Guilford Press.

Kamil, M. (2004). Vocabulary and comprehension instruction: Summary and implications of the national reading panel findings. In P. McCardle & V. Chhabra (Eds.), *The voice of evidence in reading research* (pp. 212–234). Baltimore, MD: Paul H. Brookes Publishing.

La Framboise, K. L. (2000). Saidwebs: Remedy for tired words. *The Reading Teacher, 53,* 540–546.

Martin-Chang, S. L., & Levy, B. A. (2005). Fluency transfer: Differential gains in reading speed and accuracy following isolated word and context training. *Reading and Writing, 18,* 343–376.

McKeown, J. G. & Beck, I. L. (2004). Direct and rich vocabulary instruction. In James F. Bauman & Edward J. Kame'enui (Eds.), *Vocabulary instruction: Research to practice* (pp. 13–27). New York: Guilford Press.

Nash, H., & Snowling, M. (2006). Teaching new words to children with poor existing vocabulary knowledge: A controlled evaluation of the definition and context methods. *International Journal of Language Communication Disorders, 41,* 335–354.

National Reading Panel (2000). *Report of the National Reading Panel. Teaching children to read: An evidence-based assessment of the scientific research literature on reading and its implications for reading instruction: Reports of the subgroups* (NIH Publication No. 00–4754). Washington, DC: U.S. Government Printing Office.

Ogle, D. M. (1986). K-W-L: A teaching model that develops active reading of expository text. *The Reading Teacher, 39,* 564–570.

Piercey, D. (1982). *Reading activities in content areas: An ideabook for middle and secondary schools* (2nd ed.). Boston: Allyn and Bacon.

RAND Study Group (2004). A research agenda for improving reading comprehension. In R. B. Ruddell & N. J. Unrau (Eds.), *Theoretical models and processes of reading* (5th ed.) (pp. 720–754). Newark, DE: International Reading Association.

Roberts, T., & Neal, H. (2004). Relationships among preschool English language learner's oral proficiency in English, instructional experiences and literacy development. *Contemporary Educational Psychology, 29,* 283–311.

Rupley, W., Logan, J., & Nichols, W. (1999). Vocabulary instruction in a balanced reading program. *The Reading Teacher, 52,* 336–346.

Rupley, W. H., & Nichols, W. D. (2005). Vocabulary instruction for the struggling reader. *Reading & Writing Quarterly, 21,* 239–260.

Sadoski, M. (2005). A dual coding view of vocabulary learning. *Reading & Writing Quarterly, 21,* 221–238.

Stahl, S. A., & Nagy, W. E. (2006). *Teaching word meanings.* Mahway, NJ: Erlbaum.

Vacca, J. A. L., Vacca, R. T., Gove, M. K., Burkey, L. C., Lenhart, L. A., & McKeon, C. A. (2003). *Reading and learning to read* (5th ed.). Boston: Allyn and Bacon.

# 5

# ORAL READING FLUENCY

When fifth grader Jamie curls up on her bed with a library book and begins reading to her younger sister, she could read by pausing between short phrases: "Once upon / a time / there was / a Chihuahua / named Rita, / and she / had / a friend / named Rosie." She could also pause at every word: "Once / upon / a / time / there / was / a / Chihuahua / named / Rita, /and / she / had / a / friend / named / Rosie." Likewise, she might read: "Once upon a time there was a Chihuahua named Rita, / and she had a friend named Rosie." Stopping abruptly between short oral phrases or pausing between words disrupts the natural flow of language, hinders comprehension, and interferes with enjoyment. The last option, smooth oral reading, is the kind of fluent reading we expect from a fifth grader. The best way to develop reading fluency is to have children read every day in your classroom, read at home for pleasure, read widely, and read often. In addition to wide and frequent reading, there are 17 activities to develop fluency in this chapter.

## FLUENCY CONTRIBUTES TO COMPREHENSION

Fluent reading is expressive, accurate, and appropriately paced. Fluent reading is smooth and expressive, sounds like talk, approaches the speed of normal conversation, and preserves the author's syntax. Fluent reading does not cause comprehension, but it does suggest that children understand what they read. Fluent readers make connections with text while reading; they understand what they read and interpret text in light of their prior knowledge and purpose for reading.

Generally speaking, high-fluency readers comprehend better, read faster, and read with greater accuracy than low-fluency readers (National Center for Education Statistics, 1995). High-fluency readers differ markedly from their low-fluency classmates, and these differences are readily noticeable by the fourth grade. In a nationwide study of reading fluency, the National Center for Education Statistics (NCES) found that high-fluency fourth graders read with expression and grouped words into meaningful phrases, whereas low-fluency fourth graders ignore sentence structure and read in one- or two-word phrases (1995). Fluent readers concentrate on understanding what they are reading and on reading smoothly and expressively.

## Expression

Children who read with expression have better comprehension, read faster, and read with greater accuracy than children who read word-by-word in a monotone (Daane et al., 2006). Fluent readers pay attention to punctuation and think about meaning. These readers decide where to pause and where to place emphasis and change voice tone and voice emphasis so as to make meaning clear (National Reading Panel, 2000). Expressive readers interpret meaning. They do this through the use of good phrasing, appropriate voice tone, and appropriate voice volume. A fluent reader groups words together in phrases that convey meaning, are consistent with punctuation, and correspond to sentence structure. Intonation, the second characteristic of expressive reading, is the change in voice emphasis. For instance, the reader raises the voice for question marks, slightly drops the voice for periods, puts an emphasis on words followed by exclamation marks. Volume is the use of a loud or soft voice. The child reads unimportant words in a softer voice; important words in a slightly louder voice.

## Accuracy

Generally speaking, the fewer the number of miscues, the better the comprehension; the greater the number of miscues, the poorer the comprehension (Daane et al., 2006). Choosing to correct miscues also affects comprehension. Readers who self-correct a larger percentage of miscues comprehend better than their classmates who self-correct a relatively small percentage of miscues (Daane et al., 2006).

## Rate

Reading rate affects comprehension. Information enters short-term memory before it is moved to long-term memory, where the reader stores ideas and makes sense of text. Short-term memory holds only a small amount of information and the information stays in short-term memory only a brief period of time. When the pace of reading is too slow, the reader does not move information quickly into long-term memory. Information in short-term memory creates a roadblock that prevents new information

---

**BEST PRACTICES FOR EFFECTIVE TEACHING**

1. *Give children feedback and guidance.* Feedback and guidance let children know what they do well and what they need to change. Feedback from an adult is an effective method for developing fluent reading (Heubusch & Lloyd, 1998; Therrien, 2004).

2. *Increase reading vocabulary.* Increasing reading vocabulary improves fluency and comprehension, especially when children develop vocabulary through reading a variety of text (Martin-Chang & Levy, 2005).

3. *Have children reread the same passages three or four times.* Repeated reading improves fluency. Rereading is even more effective when it is combined with other fluency-building techniques (Begeny & Silber, 2006).

4. *Establish criteria for oral reading practice.* Using performance criteria is more effective than asking children to reread the same passage for a predetermined number of times (Therrien, 2004).

5. *Use a variety of techniques to develop fluency.* Using a combination of techniques is more effective than using only a single technique (Kuhn, 2005).

6. *Give children practice reading words in context.* Practice reading words in context results in greater fluency gains than reading words in lists (Martin-Chang & Levy, 2005).

from entering, and so less information is moved on to long-term memory. Consequently, plodding readers do not grasp as many ideas as fluent readers.

## TEXT THAT MAKES IT EASIER TO DEVELOP FLUENCY

Selecting just the right text is the first step in developing fluency. Look for these types of books in your school library:

1. *Text written in natural language patterns.* The ideal text sounds like real language when read aloud (Richards, 2000).

2. *Predictable pattern books for beginners.* Predictable books use the same language pattern over and over again. Beginning readers quickly pick up the predictable pattern, and this, in turn, supports fluent reading. If you find that some children overrely on the repeated patterns and overlook text, encourage children to focus on text by asking them to show you (point to) each word as it is read. Another idea is to have a small group read in chorus and then ask individuals to read designated sentences.

3. *Rhyming poetry, limericks, and rhyming stories.* Rhyme patterns give the reader a sense of where to pause between phrases. Rhyming poetry appeals to children of all ages and is therefore a good choice for developing fluency from kindergarten through sixth grade.

4. *Lyrics to popular songs or favorite tunes.* Many songs have lyrics that support reading expressively and in phrases. Look for songs with natural language patterns. And, of course, ask children for suggestions.

5. *Plays.* Look for plays with a clear-cut plot that tells a compelling story. The lines for characters should give readers bite-size bits of text that lend themselves to oral interpretation.

See pages 125–129, "Informal Assessment or Additional Practices for Developing Oral Reading Fluency."

# ACTIVITIES

## 17 ACTIVITIES TO DEVELOP ORAL READING FLUENCY

### 5.1    Repeated Reading

- Individual
- Use to develop fluency.

In repeated reading children reread the same text several times. Repeated reading with teacher guidance and feedback improves the fluency of elementary-age children (National Reading Panel, 2000). Repeated reading also improves self-monitoring, self-correcting, and problem-solving strategies (Askew, 1993).

**Material:** Text written on instructional level that is from 50 to 100 words long, depending on the development of the reader.

**Step-by-step directions:**

1. Select text on the child's instructional level that is written in natural language patterns.
2. Ask the child to read the text three or four times.
3. Give the child guidance and feedback (Chafouleas, Martens, Dobson, Weinstein, & Gardner, 2004).

---

## 5.2   Taped Repeated Reading

- Individual
- Use to develop fluency.

The child listens to a tape of his or her own reading, assesses reading, and rereads until the child feels he or she has read fluently.

**Material:** Tape recorder; short selections just below the child's instructional level; a pencil; homemade rating scale.

**Step-by-step directions:**

1. Introduce the text and explain the taped repeated reading procedure. Agree on a goal expressed in speed and accuracy.
2. The first time the child sees a passage, have the child read it silently before reading it aloud. Thereafter the child reads and rereads the passage aloud.
3. The child is taped while reading the entire passage aloud.
4. The teacher rewinds the tape and plays back the oral reading. The child follows along in the text while listening to the tape. Listening to the taped reading gives you, the teacher, an opportunity to give feedback on the oral reading, offer tips, and guide the child in understanding what types of behaviors need improving.
5. Hand the rating scale to the child and ask, "How would you rate your own reading?" Talk about the child's self-evaluation. Repeat steps 3, 4, and 5 until the child reads fluently and the self-evaluation reflects a "Superb!" oral reading.

We use an informal scale, shown in Figure 5–1, consisting of five faces: one smiley face with the word "Superb"; one with a slight smile that says "Outstanding"; one with a straight-mouth face saying "Okay"; one with a slightly turned-down mouth that says "Not too bad"; and one with a mouth turned down a bit more that says "Not so great." The child is responsible for judging his or her own reading.

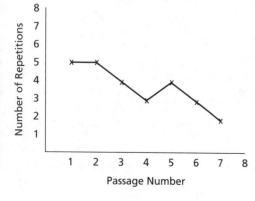

6. Graph progress. Make a simple graph, as shown. Graph how many repetitions it takes to reach fluency on each passage.
7. Send the text home with the child to share with family and friends. Since the child has practiced reading the text fluently, reading at home puts the child in the most favorable light, which builds self-confidence.

**Figure 5–1**
Taped Repeated
Reading Self-
Evaluation

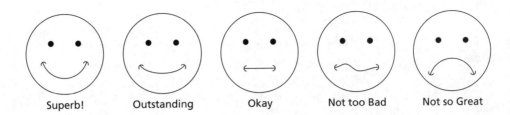

| Superb! | Outstanding | Okay | Not too Bad | Not so Great |

## 5.3 Partner Repeated Reading

- Pairs
- Use to develop fluency.

Two children take turns reading the same text several times (Koskinen & Blum, 1986).

**Material:** Passages of about 50 words.

**Step-by-step directions:**

1. Select children to work together as partners. You may select an older child to work with a younger child or a better reader to work with a weaker reader or pair children based on shared interests, such as sports, hobbies, or after-school activities.
2. Each pair selects their own material or you supply the text.
3. One child reads the passage three or four times aloud, while the other partner listens carefully. After the second, third, and fourth readings, the listening partner asks the reader several questions. The partners switch roles after the third or fourth reading.

We have used this method effectively with children up through the sixth grade with partners in the same classroom (Fox & Wright, 1997).

## 5.4 Guided Reading

- Small group
- Use to develop fluency, vocabulary, and comprehension.

Guided reading develops strategies in the context of carefully selected literature. In 2000 the National Reading Panel concluded that guided reading holds enough promise for improving fluency that it should be included in classroom reading programs.

**Material:** A copy of a book for everyone in the guided reading group.

**Step-by-step directions:**

1. Introduce the text to build enthusiasm for reading and to familiarize children with concepts, vocabulary, and language patterns that might impair comprehension and reading pleasure.

2. Children read the text individually, in small groups, or with partners.
3. Discuss with children the reading selection, reread and revisit text, and extend learning. Children may, for example, reread for certain information, discuss important ideas, discuss predictions, and explore vocabulary.
4. Informally observe the children's reading progress with an eye toward documenting their ability to read increasingly more difficult and challenging text.

Rereading text, especially in the context of developing strategies and concepts, gives children opportunities to read portions of the same text more than once, which, in turn, helps build oral reading fluency.

## 5.5    Choral Reading

- Large or small group
- Use to develop fluency.

Reading in chorus is similar to singing in chorus: Everyone joins together in a performance that blends many voices into one voice.

**Material:** Short passages or poems written in natural language patterns, divided into bite-size pieces. Rhyming poetry is well suited for choral reading. Passages with lots of dialog or that lend themselves to emotive reading are also good choices. Avoid passages that are so short that the children memorize them.

**Step-by-step directions:**

1. Model fluent reading and talk about oral interpretation.
2. The children read the selection in chorus. Children reread the selection several times until the choral reading is smooth and expressive.
3. Tape record the most fluent rereading. Play the tape for children so they can hear themselves reading.

## 5.6    Fluency Development Lesson

- Small group
- Use to develop fluency.

Fluency development lessons combine several elements of good fluency instruction (Rasinski & Padak, 2001). As described by Rasinski and Padak, these lessons are estimated to last between 10 and 15 minutes.

**Material:** Text that is from 50 to 150 words.

**Step-by-step directions:**

1. Give each child a copy of the text. As the children follow along, the teacher reads and rereads the text to model fluent reading.

2. Discuss the way you, the teacher, read with expression and good phrasing.

3. The group reads and rereads the text in chorus.

4. Children reread with a partner, using the paired repeated reading procedure.

5. Groups of two to four children perform the text for school personnel and children in other classes.

6. Special words are selected for closer study and for inclusion in children's personal word banks.

7. The children take copies of the text home to share with their families.

## 5.7    Echo Reading

- Small group or individual
- Use to develop fluency.

Echo reading gives children a model of fluent reading to imitate and an opportunity to immediately reproduce that model.

**Material:** One copy of text for every child. Short selections of narrative text with exciting dialog work best.

**Step-by-step directions:**

1. The teacher reads a sentence or a few lines aloud while a small group listens.

2. The children read the same sentence or a few lines imitating, or echoing, the teacher's fluent reading.

## 5.8    Neurological Impress

- Individual
- Use to develop fluency and increase instant-recognition vocabulary.

Neurological impress (Heckelman, 1969) is a one-on-one teaching method in which the teacher models fluent reading and the child echoes or imitates the model. The assumption is that the child develops fluency by listening to and imitating fluent reading. When first using this method, the reading materials should be on the child's easy reading level. Later, as the child develops fluency, reading materials may be moved up to the child's instructional level. According to Heckelman, vocabulary may also increase, probably due to increasing the child's exposure to words. Generally speaking, this teaching method is recommended for low-progress readers.

**Material:** Text on the child's easy reading level or instructional level, depending on the child's fluency.

**Step-by-step directions:**

1. Have the child sit next to you and just a little in front of you. Sit to the side of the child so that your mouth is close to the child's ear. Hold the book together with the child.

2. Read the text in unison. When reading aloud, you should read in a slightly louder voice and slightly ahead of the child, thereby providing a clear model for the child to follow. Track the text by moving your finger under each word as it is pronounced. Maintain a comfortable pace even when the child slows down or encounters difficulty. Do not stop when the child stumbles on a word. No sounding-out is permitted.

3. As the child becomes more fluent, the child tracks the text. If the child loses the place, you gently show the child where to track. You may even hold the child's finger while the child is tracking the words.

4. As fluency improves your voice becomes softer, thereby reducing the modeling effect. Eventually, the child's voice leads your voice in fluent reading.

## 5.9   Phrase Marking

- Individual
- Use to develop good phrasing.

Phrase marking helps the child develop the ability to read in meaningful word groups by physically marking the phrases in text. Phrases may be marked with slashes or colored highlighters. The child uses the marks on the page to practice reading in meaningful word groups.

**Material:** Two copies of text, written just below instructional level; two different-color highlighters or colored pens.

**Step-by-step directions:**

1. Preview the reading material, discuss the title, relate background information, and predict the text content.

2. Give the child a highlighter or a colored pen. Select a highlighter or pen in a different color for your own use.

3. Read the first sentence to the child. Put a slash between phrases or highlight phrases. Read the sentence again to demonstrate good phrasing. Discuss how to use punctuation and syntax as guides for grouping words into meaningful phrases.

4. Demonstrate how to group a second sentence into meaningful phrase units and demonstrate good phrasing by reading this sentence aloud.

5. The child reads the next sentence silently and uses the colored pen or highlighter to mark phrases. The child then reads the sentence aloud according to the marked phrases. Discuss how to group words into meaningful units.

6. Take turns marking phrases and reading the text in meaningful word groups. Portions of the text may be read and reread several times to practice good phrasing.

## 5.10   Readers' Theater

- Large or small group
- Use to develop fluency.

Readers' theater is a vocal dramatization of a well-rehearsed script. Little or no action accompanies the script reading; instead, the children's reading voices supply the dramatic interpretation. Sometimes minor props are used to add a little spice to the vocal dramatizations. Readers' theater improves the fluency of average (Martinez, Roser, & Strecker, 1999) and low-progress readers (Millin & Rinehart, 1999; Rinehart, 1999). Rereading occurs naturally as children prepare to perform the script for an audience.

**Material:** Plays written just below instructional level. As many scripts as there are children in the group.

**Step-by-step directions:**

1. There are many plays for all ages and reading abilities. Look for plays about a theme that is of interest to the group or corresponds to topics the children are studying.
2. Children read the text silently with a buddy or you may read the text aloud while the children follow along.
3. Children reread the play in a group, exchanging parts to get a feel for which roles they are most comfortable with and to get a sense of the characters' emotions and personalities.
4. Decide on individuals to read specific roles, based on children's preference from previous reading experiences and your understanding of the needs of the readers.
5. The children read and reread the roles, emphasizing expressive and emotive reading. Assist children with phrasing, intonation, and vocal expression.
6. Children present the play for their classmates or children in neighboring classrooms. Readers may sit, stand, or change positions while delivering the script.

There are many plays from which to choose. The following are examples of reproducible scripts: *Stories on Stage: Children's Plays for Reader's Theater (or Readers Theatre), with 15 Play Scripts from 15 Authors, Including Roald Dahl's The Twits and Louis Sachar's Sideways Stories from Wayside School* (Shepard, 2005) is a collection of fifteen plays that are adaptations of popular children's stories; *Tall Tales Read-aloud Plays* (Pugliano-Martin, 2000) is a collection of eight adaptations of traditional stories that may be integrated with social studies, math, language arts, and art in the third through the fifth grades; *Cinderella Outgrows the Glass Slipper and Other Zany Fractured Fairy Tale Plays* (Wolf, 2002) offers a selection of humorous versions of traditional fairy tales; *Revolutionary War Read-aloud Plays* (Murphy, 2000) includes five plays set during the American Revolution and appropriate for children in the fourth through eighth grades; and *5 Easy-to-Read Plays Based on Classic Stories* (Scholastic, 1999) includes adaptations of the classics appropriate for fifth-grade readers; *Readers' Theater: Sight Words: Grades 1–2* (Gerard, 2006) consists of plays that give children practice reading sight words; *25 Spanish Plays for Emergent Readers* (Pugliano-Martin & Pasternac, 1999) is a collection of plays written in Spanish for children in kindergarten and first grade; *25 Emergent Reader Plays Around the Year* (Pugliano-Martin, 1999) is a collection of plays with seasonal and holiday themes.

## 5.11     Read-Arounds

- Small group
- Use to develop fluency.

## TEACHING ENGLISH LANGUAGE LEARNERS

1. *Select books written slightly below or barely at children's level of English language proficiency.* English learners are better able to read fluently when material does not put too many demands on their knowledge of English (Geva & Zadeh, 2006).

2. *Use books for fluency development that have few infrequently used or rare words.* English language learners are less likely to know the meaning of rare or infrequently used words (Hiebert & Fisher, 2005). Look for passages with words children already know.

3. *Teach decoding and vocabulary to children who have not mastered the basic skills.* English learners are more fluent readers when they spend extra time developing word recognition and meaning vocabulary (Gunn, Smolkowski, Biglan, Black, & Blair, 2005).

4. *Try to be sensitive to the child who does not want to read aloud before a group.* Choral reading, echo reading, paired repeated reading, and readers' theater develop fluency in conditions that support English learners without singling out individuals who may not wish to read aloud by themselves (Blevins, 2005).

Read-arounds is an activity in which children share their favorite portions of a familiar selection (Tompkins, 2001). This wrap-up activity celebrates literacy through sharing and honoring children's choices and preferences.

**Material:** One copy of a familiar literature selection for each child in a small group.

**Step-by-step directions:**

1. Read and explore the text with children, following the lesson sequence that you typically use with literature.

2. The children select their favorite passages. Passages may be as short as a sentence or as long as a paragraph (Tompkins, 2001).

3. Once favorite passages are selected, the children practice or rehearse reading their favorites. Children may rehearse individually or with a buddy.

4. The children share their favorite portions with their classmates by reading the portions aloud. Children take turns reading, with reading moving from one child to another around the group, hence the name *read-arounds*. The teacher does not ask questions or interrupt the read-around. Several children may read the same passage. Favorite passages may be read in any order, with the children jumping in on their own. The teacher does not call on individuals, and children are not required to read aloud if they do not wish to do so. Teachers read their favorite passage aloud, too.

5. The read-around ends when all the children who want to share their favorite passages have read aloud to the group.

## 5.12   Tape-Assisted Reading

- Individual
- Use to develop fluency.

The child listens to a tape recording of a story or short selection and reads along with the tape.

**Material:** Tape recorder; tape of a story; a print copy of the taped story; headphones.

**Step-by-step directions:**

1. Select a tape that is age appropriate for the listener.
2. The child listens and follows along in the text, imitating the intonation, expression, and phrasing of the fluent reading.

## 5.13   News Broadcast

- Large or small group
- Use to develop fluency.

This activity was formerly called radio reading. The updated name, News Broadcast, preserves the original intent, which is to communicate with a listening audience (Searfoss, Readence, & Mallette, 2001). The focus is on communication rather than accuracy. This description is an adaptation of the original method.

**Material:** Text from literature or content textbooks or short magazine articles as appropriate for children's development as readers.

**Step-by-step directions:**

1. Each child silently reads a short section in a content-subject textbook or a content-focused magazine article.
2. Two children take turns reading the selections two or three times.
3. As pairs are reading to each other, the teacher circulates, listening to the children read. Give children feedback on oral reading, coach pairs on how to communicate with an audience, and help children identify words they do not instantly recognize.
4. Children put on a news broadcast. The goal is for the reader to communicate a message to the listeners, just as a news anchor communicates with viewers.
5. The audience listens to the reader, concentrating on understanding the message. The audience does not have a copy of the text.
6. Should listeners misunderstand the message, the confusing portions of the text are reread.
7. Children engage in a brief discussion to make sure that everyone understood the messages.

## 5.14   Group Read-Along

- Small group
- Use to develop fluency.

The teacher reads while the group follows along and then reads together in chorus. Group read-along increases the fluency and comprehension of struggling readers (Mefferd & Pettegrew, 1997).

**Material:** Text appropriate for every child in a small group; blank 3 × 5 cards.

1. *Reading Along—Day 1*  You, the teacher, read aloud while the group follows along. Individual children write words they would like to learn. The teacher writes the words on cards.
2. *Sharing Words—Day 2*  Children share their words (written on cards) with each other. You reread as children follow along.
3. *Reading Word Cards—Day 3*  Children read their word cards to the group.
4. *Reading in Chorus—Day 4*  The children and the teacher read together in chorus. Individual children may read portions of the text. The teacher draws attention to appropriate strategies.
5. *Reading Independently—Day 5*  Children read independently. The teacher confers with individuals. During the conference the teacher observes, monitors progress, and compliments each child on the use of appropriate strategies.

## 5.15    Antiphonal Choral Reading

- Large or small group
- Use to develop fluency.

An antiphon is a selection sung by groups in alterations. In antiphonal choral reading, groups take turns reading different portions of the text.

**Material:** Selections that are easily divided into bite-size pieces, such as plays, poems, or narrative text with a lot of dialog; tape recorder (optional).

**Step-by-step directions:**

1. Model fluent reading and talk about reading in phrases, with expression and at an appropriate pace.
2. Divide the group into as many sections as are present in the passage.
3. Groups read their assigned sections.
4. Repeat antiphonal choral reading until the group reads with expression and good phrasing. You may want to tape reading. Play the tape for the group. Discuss fluency. Ask children in the group to comment on the antiphonal reading.

## 5.16    Signaled Reading

- Pairs
- Use to develop fluency.

A child and fluent reader read together. The child signals when he or she wishes to read alone (Topping, 1987).

**Material:** Text written on an easy reading level.

**Step-by-step directions:**

1. A fluent reader—the teacher, parent, or adult volunteer—sits next to the child at a comfortable table or in an oversize chair. The text is placed so that both readers can see it.

2.  The adult and child agree on a signal the child will use to tell the fluent reader to stop reading.

3.  The adult and child read together.

4.  The adult pronounces words the child does not recognize. Reading resumes after the child reads the word correctly.

5.  At a signal from the child the adult stops reading aloud. The child continues reading aloud while the adult reads silently.

6.  The child continues reading until he or she misreads a word or hesitates several seconds before reading a word. The adult pronounces the word.

7.  The child reads the word correctly.

8.  The adult and child resume reading together until the child signals for the adult to read silently while the child reads aloud.

## 5.17     Phrased Reading

- Small group
- Use to develop good phrasing.

A small group reads poems or short selections in phrases.

**Material:** Familiar poems or short selections written in natural language patterns.

**Step-by-step directions:**

1.  Write each line (or phrases if lines consist of more than one phrase) on a sentence strip.

2.  Show the children the strips one at a time. The children read the selection phrase-by-phrase.

3.  Fasten the sentences (or phrases) to a large chart paper. Practice reading in chorus, calling attention to the sentences (or phrases) on separate strips.

## INFORMAL ASSESSMENT OR ADDITIONAL PRACTICES FOR DEVELOPING ORAL READING FLUENCY

### Additional Practices

*Modeling and coaching.* Modeling gives children a representation of fluent reading to imitate. Coaching gives children feedback on their oral reading. You will be more effective at modeling fluency when you:

1.  Tell children you are going to show them how you read fluently.

2.  Read a relatively short passage to keep children's attention.

3.  Give children practice, under your guidance, immediately following modeling.

If children have difficulty imitating your model, try modeling only one characteristic of fluent reading at a time, such as expression, phrasing, or reading at an appropriate pace.

*Shared reading.* Shared reading is appropriate for beginning readers. Shared reading includes teacher modeling, repeated reading, and opportunities for even the youngest readers to successfully imitate fluency. While shared reading has many advantages, the particular benefit for fluency development is that children's first oral reading experiences are modeled on the fluent reading of their teacher and, therefore, reflect the habits and behaviors of fluent readers.

*Language experience.* Language experience is appropriate for beginning readers. Children dictate stories and then read them. Children and their teacher reread portions of the text together, and the children read and reread all, or part, of the text individually. Repeated reading of familiar text written in children's own language about their own experiences is expected to help children develop greater fluency.

*Reading a variety of texts.* The type of text may affect the reader's fluency. Children need to develop fluency reading more than one genre. Encourage fluency reading different types of text by giving lots of practice reading texts like mathematics books, science texts, essays, and magazine articles. Children also benefit from watching you model reading different types of text and benefit from coaching that gives them feedback and guidance on their own fluency.

## Informal Assessment in the Classroom

Most informal measures of fluency are holistic; that is, we listen for an overall impression of the child's ability to read with expression, accuracy, and at an appropriate pace.

*Informal Reading Inventories (IRIs).* Informal reading inventories are collections of passages the child reads orally and silently. The teacher notes accuracy and comprehension. The quality of the child's reading is used to identify the level of text that is suitable for independent reading and instruction and the level of text that is too difficult. Informal inventories do not provide us with a fluency score. However, some inventories do indicate whether the child's reading rate is appropriate. Additionally, as we listen to the child read we can judge the child's fluency reading text at different levels.

*Running records and miscue analysis.* These two informal assessments identify the strategies the child uses while reading and determine the child's development as a reader. Running records and miscue analysis differ, but both include the child reading aloud and the teacher judging whether miscues change meaning, have the same or different syntactic properties as the correct word, or are visually similar or different from the correct word. The running record procedure uses the percentage of miscues to determine the child's ability to read text at a certain difficulty level. After reading, the child may retell the story or passage. Accurate retelling indicates good comprehension. Neither informal assessment gives us a fluency rating. However, we can use the opportunity to make holistic judgments of the child's fluency.

*Fluency scale.* The National Assessment of Educational Progress (NAEP) uses a four-level scale to evaluate fluency (Daane et al., 2006). Levels 4 and 3 are gradations of fluent reading; levels 1 and 2 are gradations of nonfluent reading. NAEP assessed the expressive reading of fourth graders in 2002. Evaluators listened to individual children read and rated fluency based on their overall impression of the reader's expression. See Figure 5–2 for a description of the NAEP four-level scale. Use this fluency scale to guide you in evaluating the child's oral reading. Find text written on the child's instructional level. Select text the child has not seen before. Ask the child to read aloud. Listen for an overall impression of the child's expressive reading.

**Figure 5–2**
Oral Reading
Fluency Scale

### FLUENT READING

#### Level 4

Level 4 is characterized by smooth and expressive reading using large, meaningful phrases. When Level 4 readers miscue, their misreadings do not affect text meaning and do not detract from the overall intent of the author. Nationally, 10 percent of fourth graders read at Level 4.

#### Level 3

The child uses three- and four-word phrases, along with a few smaller word groupings. While Level 3 phrasing is generally appropriate and preserves text meaning, the child reads with little or no expression. The largest portion of fourth graders, 51 percent nationwide, read at this level.

### NONFLUENT READING

#### Level 2

At Level 2 the child primarily reads in two-word phrases, along with some three- and four-word phrases. Phrasing is awkward and unrelated to text meaning. The child does not read with expression. Thirty-two percent of fourth graders are in this category.

#### Level 1

Level 1, the poorest level, is characterized by word-by-word reading. Phrases, should they occur, are not consistent with meaning. Nationally, 8 percent of fourth graders read at this level.

*Adapted from: The Nation's Report Card: Fourth-grade Students Reading Aloud: NAEP 2002 Special Study of Oral Reading, by M. C. Daane, J. R. Campbell, W. S. Grigg, M. J. Goodman, A. Orange, & A. Goldstein, 2006, Washington, DC: U.S. Department of Education, Institute of Education Statistics (NCES 2006-469).*

*Oral reading fluency (ORF).* Oral reading fluency (ORF) is the number of words correctly read in 1 minute. The more words the child accurately and automatically recognizes, the faster the rate and the better the oral reading fluency. Use ORF scores to track reading development throughout the year (Fuchs, Fuchs, Hosp, & Jenkins, 2001; Speece & Ritchey, 2005). Table 5–1 shows ORF norms for the beginning, middle, and end of the year for children in Grades 1 through 8 (Hasbrouck & Tindal, 2006). Follow these steps to assess oral reading fluency:

1. Select a passage written at an instructional level that the child has not read before.

2. Ask the child to read aloud.

3. Record miscues.

4. Put a slash beside the last word read at 60 seconds.

5. Count the number of words the child read in a minute.

6. Subtract the number of miscues from the words read per minute to determine Oral Reading Fluency.

    number of words − miscues = correct words read per minute (WCPM)

    For example, if Liza read 150 words in 60 seconds with 3 miscues, we would calculate the following:

    150 words read − 3 miscues = 147 ORF

We use the acronym WPM (words per minute) to express the total number of words read in 1 minute. In our example, Liza read 150 words in 1 minute (WPM). We use the acronym WCPM (words correct per minute) to express the number of correct words

**TABLE 5–1  Oral reading fluency norms, grades 1–8**

| Grade | Percentile | WCPM Fall | WCPM Winter | WCPM Spring |
|---|---|---|---|---|
| 1 | 90 | | 81 | 111 |
| | 75 | | 47 | 82 |
| | 50 | | 23 | 53 |
| | 25 | | 12 | 28 |
| | 10 | | 6 | 15 |
| | SD | | 32 | 39 |
| | Count | | 16,950 | 19,434 |
| 2 | 90 | 106 | 125 | 142 |
| | 75 | 79 | 100 | 117 |
| | 50 | 51 | 72 | 89 |
| | 25 | 25 | 42 | 61 |
| | 10 | 11 | 18 | 31 |
| | SD | 37 | 41 | 42 |
| | Count | 15,896 | 18,229 | 20,128 |
| 3 | 90 | 128 | 146 | 162 |
| | 75 | 99 | 120 | 137 |
| | 50 | 71 | 92 | 107 |
| | 25 | 44 | 62 | 78 |
| | 10 | 21 | 36 | 48 |
| | SD | 40 | 43 | 44 |
| | Count | 16,988 | 17,383 | 18,372 |
| 4 | 90 | 145 | 166 | 180 |
| | 75 | 119 | 139 | 152 |
| | 50 | 94 | 112 | 123 |
| | 25 | 68 | 87 | 98 |
| | 10 | 45 | 61 | 72 |
| | SD | 40 | 41 | 43 |
| | Count | 16,523 | 14,572 | 16,269 |
| 5 | 90 | 166 | 182 | 194 |
| | 75 | 139 | 156 | 168 |
| | 50 | 110 | 127 | 139 |
| | 25 | 85 | 99 | 109 |
| | 10 | 61 | 74 | 83 |
| | SD | 45 | 44 | 45 |
| | Count | 16,212 | 13,331 | 15,292 |
| 6 | 90 | 177 | 195 | 204 |
| | 75 | 153 | 167 | 177 |
| | 50 | 127 | 140 | 150 |
| | 25 | 98 | 111 | 122 |
| | 10 | 68 | 82 | 93 |
| | SD | 42 | 45 | 44 |
| | Count | 10,520 | 9,218 | 11,290 |
| 7 | 90 | 180 | 192 | 202 |
| | 75 | 156 | 165 | 177 |
| | 50 | 128 | 136 | 150 |
| | 25 | 102 | 109 | 123 |

**TABLE 5–1** *(Continued)*

| Grade | Percentile | WCPM Fall | WCPM Winter | WCPM Spring |
|-------|-----------|-----------|-------------|-------------|
|       | 10        | 79        | 88          | 98          |
|       | SD        | 40        | 43          | 41          |
|       | Count     | 6,482     | 4,058       | 5,998       |
| 8     | 90        | 185       | 199         | 199         |
|       | 75        | 161       | 173         | 177         |
|       | 50        | 133       | 146         | 151         |
|       | 25        | 106       | 115         | 124         |
|       | 10        | 77        | 84          | 97          |
|       | SD        | 43        | 45          | 41          |
|       | Count     | 5,546     | 3,495       | 5,335       |

WCPM: Words correct per minute

SD: Standard deviation

Count: Number of student scores

Source: From "Oral Reading Fluency Norms: A Valuable Assessment Tool for Reading Teachers," by J. Hasbrouck, & G. A. Tindal, 2006, *The Reading Teacher, 59*, pp. 636–644.

Liza read in a minute. Liza read 147 WCPM. WCPM gives us a better idea of Liza's ability to read the passage with both speed and accuracy. The number of WCPM represents Oral Reading Fluency (ORF).

## FLUENCY IN THE CLASSROOM

### Kindergarten, First, and Second Grades

Kindergartners hear models of fluent reading when adults and the teacher read storybooks aloud. Kindergartners produce a facsimile of fluent reading when they pretend to read familiar storybooks. In kindergarten and at the beginning of first grade, teachers use shared reading to introduce children to reading connected text. These early reading experiences contribute to the child's concept of how fluent reading sounds.

Fluent reading is taught throughout first and second grades. Most classroom programs teach fluency at least once a week, though some programs teach fluency more than this. Children reread text, read with partners, and participate in readers' theater. Teachers model fluency by showing children how to read with expression, with accuracy, and at a pace that approximates speech. Teachers also coach children by giving children feedback on their oral reading.

### Third, Fourth, Fifth, and Sixth Grades

Third through sixth graders read silently most of the time, but even though children spend most of their time reading silently, oral reading fluency is still important. Fluency modeling and coaching continue to be important teaching tools in these grades. By the time children leave the sixth grade, they read story and informational text fluently. They read effortlessly, at an appropriate rate, and with engaging expression that captivates the listener.

## WORKING WITH CHILDREN AT RISK

1. *Select passages with some vocabulary control.* At-risk children who read text with many shared words make fluency gains in almost half the time as children who read text with unusual words, long words, and few repeated words (Hiebert, 2005; Rashotte & Torgesen, 1985).

2. *Ask an adult to give children feedback.* Feedback from adults is more effective than feedback from classmates (Chalfouleas, Martens, Dobson, Weinstein, & Gardner, 2004; Therrien, 2004).

3. *Encourage and support wide reading.* Wide reading and repeated reading improve the ability of children at risk to read accurately and with expression (Kuhn, 2005).

4. *Select books on the same topic.* Fluency improves when at-risk children read books on the same topic with many of the same words (Hiebert, 2005).

# REFERENCES

Askew, B. J. (1993). The effect of multiple readings on the behaviors of children and teachers in an early intervention program. *Reading and Writing Quarterly: Overcoming Learning Difficulties, 9,* 307–315.

Begeny, J. C., & Silber, J. M. (2006). An examination of group-based treatment packages for increasing elementary-aged students' reading fluency. *Psychology in the Schools, 43,* 183–195.

Blevins, W. (2005). The importance of reading fluency and the English language learner. *The Language Teacher, 29,* 13–16.

Chalfouleas, S. M., Martens, B. K., Dobson, R. L., Weinstein, K. S., & Gardner, K. B. (2004). Fluent reading as the improvement stimulus control: Additive effects of performance-based interventions to repeated reading on students' reading and error rates. *Journal of Behavioral Education, 13,* 67–81.

Daane, M. C., Campbell, J. R., Grigg, W. S., Goodman, M. J., Orange, A., & Goldstein, A. (2006). *The nation's report card: Fourth-grade students reading aloud: NAEP 2002 special study of oral reading.* Washington, DC: U.S. Department of Education, Institute of Education Statistics (NCES 2006-469).

Fox, B. J., & Wright, M. P. (1997). Connecting school and home literacy experiences through cross-age reading. *The Reading Teacher, 50,* 382–403.

Fuchs, L. S., Fuchs, D., Hosp, M. K., & Jenkins, J. R. (2001). Oral reading fluency as an indication of reading competence: A theoretical, empirical, and historical analysis. *Scientific Studies of Reading, 5,* 239–256.

Gerard, M. (2006). *Reader's theater: Sight words: Grades 1–2.* Westminster, CA: Teacher Created Resources.

Geva, E., & Zadeh, Z. Y. (2006). Reading efficiency in native English speaking and English-as-a-second language children: The role of oral proficiency and underlying cognitive-linguistic processes. *Scientific Studies of Reading, 10,* 31–57.

Gunn, B., Smolkowski, K., Biglan, A., Black, C., & Blair, J. (2005). Fostering development of reading skill through supplemental instruction: Results for Hispanic and Nonhispanic students. *The Journal of Special Education, 39,* 66–85.

Hasbrouck, J., & Tindal, G. A. (2006). Oral reading fluency norms: A valuable assessment tool for reading teachers. *The Reading Teacher, 59,* 636–644.

Heckelman, R. B. (1969). Neurological impress method of remedial reading instruction. *Academic Therapy Quarterly, 4,* 277–282.

Heubusch, J. D., & Lloyd, J. W. (1998). Corrective feedback on oral reading. *Journal of Behavioral Education, 8,* 63–79.

Hiebert, E. H. (2005). The effects of text difficulty on second graders' fluency development. *Reading Psychology, 26,* 183–209.

Hiebert, E. H., & Fisher, C. W. (2005). A review of the National Reading Panel's studies on fluency: The role of text. *The Elementary School Journal, 105,* 443–460.

Koskinen, P., & Blum, I. (1986). Paired repeated reading: A classroom strategy for developing fluent reading. *The Reading Teacher, 40,* 70–75.

Kuhn, M. R. (2005). A comparative study of small group fluency instruction. *Reading Psychology, 26*, 127–140.

Martin-Chang, S. L., & Levy, B. A. (2005). Fluency transfer: Differential gains in reading speed and accuracy following isolated word and context training. *Reading and Writing, 18*, 343–376.

Martinez, M., Roser, N. L., & Strecker, S. (1999). "I never thought I could be a star": A readers theatre ticket to fluency. *The Reading Teacher, 52*, 326–334.

Mefferd, P. E., & Pettegrew, B. S. (1997). Fostering literacy acquisition of students with developmental disabilities: Assisted reading with predictable trade books. *Reading Research and Instruction, 36*, 177–190.

Millin, S., & Rinehart, S. D. (1999). Some of the benefits of readers theater participation for second-grade title I students. *Reading Research and Instruction, 39*, 71–88.

Murphy, D. (2000). *Revolutionary war read-aloud plays*. New York: Scholastic.

National Center for Education Statistics (1995). Listening to children read aloud: Oral reading fluency. Retrieved March 10, 2007 from http://nces.ed.gov/pubs95/web/95762.asp

National Reading Panel (2000). *Report of the national reading panel. Teaching children to read: An evidence-based assessment of the scientific research literature on reading and its implications for reading instruction: Reports of the subgroups* (NIH Publication No. 00-4754). Washington, DC: U.S. Government Printing Office.

Pugliano-Martin, C. (1999). 25 emergent reader plays around the year. New York: Scholastic.

Pugliano-Martin, C. (2000). *Tall tales read-aloud plays*. New York: Scholastic.

Pugliano-Martin, C., & Pasternac, S. (1999). *25 Spanish Plays for Emergent Readers*. New York: Scholastic.

Rashotte, C. A. & Torgesen, J. K. (1985). Repeated reading and reading fluency in learning disabled children. *Reading Research Quarterly, 20*, 180–188.

Rasinski, T. V., & Padak, N. D. (2001). *From phonics to fluency: Effective teaching of decoding and reading fluency in the elementary school*. New York: Longman.

Richards, M. (2000). Be a good detective: Solve the case of oral reading fluency. *The Reading Teacher, 53*, 534–539.

Rinehart, S.D. (1999). "Don't think for a minute that I'm getting up there:" Opportunities for readers' theater in a tutorial for children with reading problems. *Journal of Reading Psychology, 20*, 71–89.

Scholastic. (1999). *5 easy-to-read plays based on classic stories*. New York: Scholastic.

Searfoss, L. W., Readence, J. E., & Mallette, M. H. (2001). *Helping children learn to read: Creating a classroom literacy environment*. Boston: Allyn and Bacon.

Shepard, A. (2005). *Stories on stage: Children's plays for reader's theater (or readers theatre), with 15 play scripts from 15 authors, including Roald Dahl's The Twits and Louis Sachar's Sideways Stories from Wayside School*. Olympia, WA: Shepard Publications.

Speece, D. L., & Ritchey, K. D. (2005). A longitudinal study of the development of oral reading fluency in young children at risk for reading failure. *Journal of Learning Disabilities, 38*, 387–399.

Therrien, W. J. (2004). Fluency and comprehension gains as a result of repeated reading: A meta-analysis. *Remedial and Special Education, 25*(4), 252–261.

Tompkins, G. E. (2001). *Literacy for the 21st century: A balanced approach* (2nd ed.). Columbus, OH: Merrill.

Topping, K. (1987). Paired reading: A powerful technique for parent use. *The Reading Teacher, 40*, 608–614.

Wolf, J. M. (2002). *Cinderella outgrows the glass slipper and other zany fractured fairy tale plays*. New York: Scholastic.

# 6

# COMPREHENSION

Monica is reading a report she wrote on the Lewis and Clark expedition. She reads accurately, with expression, in meaningful phrases, and at an appropriate rate. Monica gathered information for her report from books in the library and online websites. She used many strategies to prepare her report. She decided which facts were important and which were not. She related her background knowledge to text, set purposes for reading references, drew conclusions, and summarized. She also judged the credibility of online websites with her teacher's help.

## FLUENT READING OPENS THE DOOR TO COMPREHENSION

Fluency and comprehension are related and interact (Chard, Pikulski, & McDonagh, 2006). Although the exact extent and nature of this interaction is not well understood, there is reason to believe that comprehension informs fluency at some level. Similarly, fluency affects comprehension by making it possible for the reader to pay attention to meaning. Fluent readers learn more with less effort, read more text, complete homework in less time, and have higher achievement than nonfluent readers (Joshi, 2005).

Nonfluent readers miss information that fluent readers grasp. Missing information is less problematic when the text is a good match for readers' life experiences, more problematic when text introduces unfamiliar ideas and concepts. By and large, text for first and second graders does not stray far from children's background knowledge. Even though nonfluent readers in these grades miss information, some children still have good comprehension. These children understand text because they use their background knowledge to fill in the gaps in information. As children move into the third and fourth grades the text begins to introduce new ideas, information, and concepts. Nonfluent readers who got by in first and second grade begin to struggle with reading in the third grade. By the fourth grade most nonfluent readers have fallen far behind their classmates.

Fluent readers have high standards for comprehension. They monitor their own reading to keep track of meaning. When comprehension breaks down, they use fix-up strategies to pick up the thread of meaning. Fluent readers multitask. They recognize words, note punctuation, regulate reading pace, group words into phrases, change voice tone to match meaning, and comprehend text at nearly the same time. Fluent readers can multitask because they carry out the processes that support fluency automatically without conscious awareness. Consequently, fluent readers spend their mental resources on thinking about meaning and connecting with the text.

## COMPREHENSION STRATEGIES

Fluent readers use their background knowledge or prior knowledge to help them make sense of text. As it turns out, prior knowledge is a foot in the door to comprehension. Readers check text content against their own knowledge of the world and interpret text within the framework of their existing knowledge. When text introduces new information and concepts, readers adjust their thinking to accommodate the new ideas.

All text follows a certain structure. Understanding how text is structured makes it possible for readers to know where to find information and how to organize their thinking. Setting purposes for reading and asking questions guide readers to identify the main idea and supporting facts. Identifying the main idea makes it possible for readers to organize facts and details, determine which facts and details are important and which are not, and to summarize. Summarizing, in turn, improves children's ability to remember what they read (Thiede & Anderson, 2003; Trabasso & Bouchard, 2002).

Children also learn to identify and understand cause-and-effect relationships. These relationships are particularly important because readers cannot make inferences if they do not understand cause and effect. Children make inferences by combining information directly stated in the text with their background knowledge. Whereas fluent readers use the facts, ideas, and concepts in text to make inferences, nonfluent readers

---

**BEST PRACTICES FOR EFFECTIVE TEACHING**

1. *Demonstrate comprehension strategies and tell children when they successfully use strategies.* Modeling strategy use and telling children when they successfully apply strategies results in better reading (Bimmel, 2001; Chapman & Tunmer, 2003).

2. *Ask "how do you know this answer?"* Explaining answers also creates opportunities to draw distinctions between prior knowledge and what the text says (Brandão & Oakhill, 2005; Zinar, 2005).

3. *Teach the structure of informational text.* Teaching children to recognize the structure of informational text improves comprehension and is more effective than only teaching text content (Hall, Sabey, & McClellan, 2005; Williams, et al., 2005).

4. *Develop reading vocabulary.* There is a strong connection between reading vocabulary and comprehension. Children with a large reading vocabulary are more likely to be fluent readers who spend more time reading and learning from text (Harmon, Hedrick, & Wood, 2005; Joshi, 2005; National Reading Panel, 2000).

5. *Have young children use objects to show the action in sentences.* Give children in the early grades objects that represent events in the text they are reading. Have them move the objects to show actions and meaning. Showing meaning in this way results in better comprehension than rereading sentences (Glenberg, Gutierrez, Levin, Japuntich, & Kaschak, 2004).

6. *Try to have children work together in pairs or in small groups whenever feasible.* Cooperative learning improves comprehension (National Reading Panel, 2000; Trabasso & Bouchard, 2002).

appear to do this only when the text has specific questions that ask for an inference. Difficulty making inferences results in poor comprehension, even when children have adequate prior knowledge. In addition to understanding implied information, children think critically about the text and its relevance to their lives. Children might draw conclusions, evaluate text, or judge authors' credibility. Fluent readers also pay close attention to comprehension. They monitor their own comprehension to make sure they understand text, pause to sort out meaning when text does not make sense, and then take action to get comprehension back on track.

# ACTIVITIES

## 16 ACTIVITIES TO DEVELOP COMPREHENSION

### 6.1    Main Idea, Fact, or Detail Handprint

- Small group or pairs
- Use with information text for finding the main idea and identifying important facts and details.

**Figure 6–1**
Main Idea, Fact, or Detail Handprint

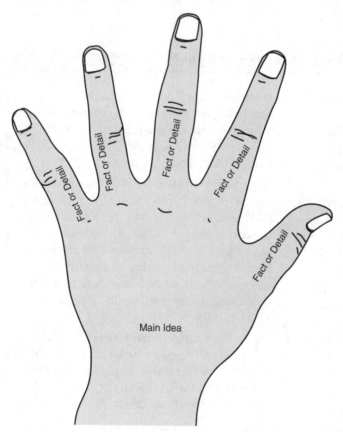

Children draw an outline of their hand and then write the main idea, facts, and details on the print.

**Material:** Paper; pencils.

**Step-by-step directions:**

1. Read and discuss a selection. Think aloud—share your thoughts—as you model how to find the main idea, facts, or details.

2. Have children read a selection to identify the main idea, facts, or details.

3. Ask children to draw an outline of their hands or you may want to draw a handprint and distribute it to the children.

4. Children write the main idea on the palm, the facts and details on the fingers (Figure 6–1).

5. Ask children to read another short selection. Then have them work with a partner to fill out a second handprint.

6. Children share the second handprint with others in the group.

# 6.2 Who, What, Where, and When Sentence Sorting

- Pairs, individual, or learning center
- Use for identifying the important details of who, what, where, and when.

**Material:** Sentences from familiar text; scissors; envelopes.

**Step-by-step directions:**

1. Write three or four sentences on the board. Model how to find the words or phrases that indicate who, what, where, and when. Underline the words and write who, what, where, or when underneath.

<u>Yesterday</u> <u>the puppy and I</u> <u>played</u> <u>in the yard</u>.
   when         who       what      where

2. Give children a sheet of paper with sentences spaced widely apart, a pair of scissors, and four envelopes. Children read the sentences and look for information that tells who, what, where, and when.

**Figure 6–2**
Who, What, When, and Where Sort

Directions:

1. Write *who* on one envelope, *what* on a second envelope, *where* on a third envelope, and *when* on a fourth envelope.
2. Read each sentence. Cut the sentences into words groups that tell who, what, where and when.

Mary / got a puppy / at the animal shelter / last Saturday.

Every morning / I / eat a bowl of cereal / in the kitchen.

| Who | What |
|---|---|
| Mary | got a puppy |

| Where | When |
|---|---|
| at the animal shelter | last Saturday |

| Who | What |
|---|---|
| I | eat a bowl of cereal |

| Where | When |
|---|---|
| at the kitchen table. | every morning |

3. Have the children write who, what, where, and when on four different envelopes.
4. Children cut each sentence into words that tell who, what, where, and when, and place the words in the correct envelopes (Figure 6–2).

## 6.3   Snapshots

- Large group, small group, or pairs
- Use for remembering facts and details.

Pairs illustrate portions of a story; the group reads the entire story and compares illustrations with story content.

**Material:** One copy of a story that is cut into one- or two-page sections; a copy of the entire story for everyone in the group; paper; crayons, markers, or pencils.

**Step-by-step directions:**

1. Cut a story into single pages. Give pairs one or two pages.
2. Pairs read the pages, discuss events, and illustrate important facts, details, and events.
3. Ask everyone in the group to read the entire story silently.
4. After reading the pairs tape pictures together to re-create the story.
5. Call on pairs to use the pictures to tell the story.
6. Compare the pictures with the facts, details, and events in the actual story. Do the illustrations accurately portray the story events? Is all the important information depicted?
7. Write on the board important facts, details, or events that need to be added to the illustrations.
8. Children add elements to pictures only when important facts, details, or events have been omitted.

## 6.4   Main Idea Map

- Large group, small group, pairs, or individual
- Use for finding the main idea.

Readers develop an understanding of how the main idea is elaborated through examples and details.

**Materials:** Text for each child; chart paper; markers.

**Step-by-step directions:**

1. Have children read a selection to identify the main idea and related details.
2. During reading, ask children to stop at predetermined places in the text that present the main idea, examples, or details.
3. After reading, ask the children to state the main idea. Write it on the board.

**Figure 6–3**
Main Idea Map

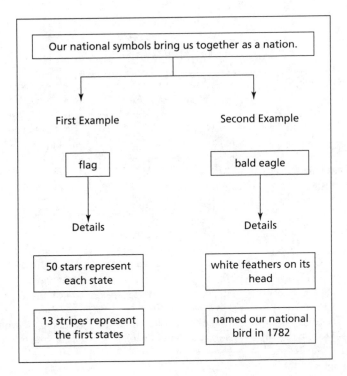

4. Ask children to find details or examples; write the details or examples on the board to create a main idea map (Figure 6–3).

5. Model how to differentiate important details from not-so-important details.

6. Have pairs read another short selection. Children make their own main idea and detail maps on chart paper. Pairs share their maps with others in the class or group. Figure 6–3 shows a map for national symbols.

## 6.5    Tic-Tac-Toe

- Small group
- Use for finding details or information that support inferences.

**Material:** One copy of familiar text for each child; a tic-tac-toe figure on the board with questions or inferences written in the squares.

**Step-by-step directions:**

1. Draw a tic-tac-toe figure on the board. Write a fact question from familiar text in each of the nine squares or write an inference in the squares (Figure 6–4).

2. Divide a small group into two teams. One team is the Xs, the other the Os.

3. The first team chooses a fact question or an inference.

4. If the team locates the correct answer within the time you specify, the team puts an X or an O in the square.

5. Teams alternate choosing questions and locating answers until one team wins or so many squares are filled that it is not possible for a team to get three Xs or three Os diagonally, vertically, or horizontally.

**Figure 6–4**
Comprehension
Tic-Tac-Toe

### Inference Tic-Tac-Toe
### The Three Little Pigs

| | | |
|---|---|---|
| The wolf was hungry. | The straw house was flimsy. | The brick house was sturdy. |
| A brick house is stronger than a straw house. | The wolf was full of pride. | The stick house was flimsy. |
| The third little pig was smarter than the wolf. | The first little pig thought he was safe from the wolf. | The third little pig was clever. |

### Fact Tic-Tac-Toe
### The Three Little Pigs

| | | |
|---|---|---|
| What did the first little pig use to build his house? | What did the second little pig use to build his house? | What happened to the straw house? |
| What happened to the stick house? | What did the third little pig use to build his house? | What did the wolf say when he came to the stick house? |
| What happened to the second little pig? | What did the third little pig use to build his house? | What happened to the third little pig? |

## 6.6   Herringbone

- Small group
- Use for main idea and important details, or cause and effect.

Herringbone is a sketch of a fish skeleton that serves as an outline for identifying and remembering facts, details, and the main idea.

**Material:** A herringbone pattern for each child; text for each child; two short reading selections—one for whole group modeling and one for children to complete in pairs.

**Figure 6–5**
Main Idea, Facts and Details Herringbone

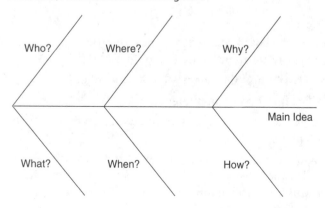

**Step-by-step directions:**

1. Draw a herringbone on the board (Figure 6–5). Explain that children write who, what, when, where, how, and why on the "bones."
2. Model how to combine who, what, where, when, why, and how information into a main idea statement.
3. Use a short selection to model how to find answers to the five W questions and how to state the main idea.
4. Give pairs a herringbone illustration and reading selection.

**Figure 6–6**
Cause and Effect Herringbone

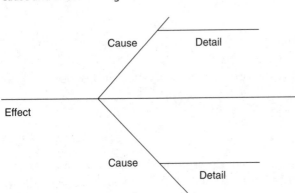

5. Children read the selection and complete the herringbone under your guidance.
6. When pairs have completed the herringbone, draw another herringbone on the board, discuss the information children found, and write information on the herringbone (Figure 6–5).
7. Talk about the idea that some passages do not give us all the who, what, where, when, and why information in the herringbone.
8. Figure 6.6 shows a herringbone for cause and effect with supporting details.

## 6.7    ReQuest

- Small group or individual
- Use for self-questioning, finding facts and details, and setting purposes.

The teacher and children take turns asking and answering questions about instructional-level text (Manzo, 1969). The teacher models asking questions and helps readers learn to phrase questions. Originally intended for one-to-one, ReQuest can be adapted for small groups and is appropriate for children who lag behind their classmates in comprehension.

**Material:** One copy of the text for each reader.

**Step-by-step directions:**

In this example we use ReQuest with a small group. The steps are the same when reading with a single child.

1. Discuss the title and illustrations. Explain that you and the reader will read a sentence at a time and take turns asking each other questions.
2. Set a purpose for reading.
3. Designate a portion of the text to read first.
4. The teacher and children read silently. Then the teacher closes the book and calls on a child to ask a question. Asking questions gives children practice framing questions and gives you the opportunity to coach children on good question-asking behavior.
5. The children and teacher open their books and read another portion of the text. After reading, the children close their books and the teacher asks a question. The teacher models how to ask good questions and demonstrates the self-questioning strategy. Try to ask questions that draw on information in several sentences or paragraphs.
6. Continue taking turns asking and answering questions until enough text has been read to set a purpose for reading.
7. After establishing a purpose, the children read silently.
8. Discuss the text after the children have finished reading.

## 6.8    Advertisements

- Small group
- Use for making inferences.

Children use the clues in advertising text to infer the product the text describes.

**Material:** Advertisements cut in two pieces; marker.

**Step-by-step directions:**

1. Locate advertisements in magazines or descriptions in catalogs. Cut the advertisements out of the magazines and cut them in two pieces: One piece shows the picture and the other the descriptive text. Give each picture and matching text the same number, writing the number on the back of the picture. It is important that the number on the back of the picture does not show through the paper. Avoid this by using a light-color marker or putting a small sticky note with a number on the back.
2. Give the children the text only. Put the pictures in the chalk tray.
3. Pairs decide which product the text describes and write the name on a piece of paper.
4. Call on pairs to read the text to the class, name the article, and give the reasons they think the text describes the article.
5. Then the pairs find the picture of the article on the chalk tray. If the numbers of the picture and text match, the children sit down. If the numbers do not match, model how to infer the product's identity or ask class members to suggest a product. Children should give their reasons for matching the product with the text.

## 6.9    Predicting Events and Sequencing with Comic Strips

- Small group, pairs, or individual
- Use for making predictions or sequencing.

Children make predictions from frames of a comic strip or arrange frames in sequence.

**Material:** Comic strips.

**Step-by-step directions:**

**Predicting Events**

1. Show children a comic strip with the last frame removed and have children predict the event in the final frame.
2. Write predictions on the board.
3. Show children the last frame. Talk about using information in text combined with our background knowledge to predict events. Also point out that (1) not all predictions are correct, (2) it is important to use what we know to guess

upcoming events, (3) when we read the text we find out if our predictions were correct, and (4) we may change our predictions when we have more information about the text.

### Sequencing

1. Give individuals or pairs comic strips cut into frames.
2. Children arrange the frames in sequence.
3. Have children trade comic strip frames and sequence the new frames for more practice.

## 6.10   Graphic Organizers

- Large group, small group, or pairs
- Use to make connections among concepts, information in the text and background knowledge.

The children and the teacher construct a graphic display showing relationships among concepts and information the children are reading. Graphic organizers are an evidence-based strategy (National Reading Panel, 2000).

**Material:** Chart paper and markers.

**Step-by-step directions:**

Structured overviews may be constructed before or after reading.

1. Write a word that labels a concept on the board.
2. Children brainstorm to think of everything they know about the concept. Write this information on the board.

**Figure 6–7**
Graphic Organizer for Clouds

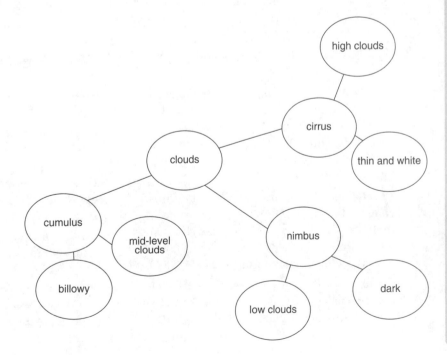

3. After children have read a selection, the group adds information and relationships described in the text.

4. Discuss how to arrange the information, ideas, and concepts to show connections. This creates a hierarchical display in which each entry is linked to the major concept. In Figure 6–7, the major concept is that there are different types of clouds.

5. Once you are certain that children understand how to display connections and hiercharchal relationships, have small groups of three construct their own organizers for a selection on a large piece of chart paper.

6. Display organizers. Share them with the larger group. Talk about connections among ideas, concepts, and information.

## 6.11    Murals

- Large group or small group
- Use for story structure, for sequence of events or to develop mental images of important story.

Murals encourage children to create images of text meaning. They are also a useful tool for introducing vocabulary, the story setting, and important facts and relationships about a somewhat unfamiliar topic (McKenzie, & Danielson, 2003). Creating mental images is a research-validated teaching practice (National Reading Panel, 2000).

**Material:** Chart paper cut into sections; colored markers or crayons; black markers.

**Step-by-step directions:**

1. Read and discuss a story or a portion of information text (social studies, for example) the children are reading. Encourage children to visualize the scenes, the setting, characters, interactions, problem and solution in a story, or the events in a social studies text they are reading.

2. Have small groups of two to four children draw one scene or social studies event.

### TEACHING ENGLISH LANGUAGE LEARNERS

1. *Develop English language proficiency.* Knowing more English words is related to better comprehension (Carlisle & Beeman, 2000; Hutchinson, Whiteley, Smith, & Connors, 2003; Miller, Heilmann, Nockerts, Iglesias, & Fabiano, 2006).

2. *Develop vocabulary in the child's home language.* Children who know many words in their first language comprehend English text better than children with less knowledge (Proctor, Carlo, August, & Snow, 2006).

3. *Combine writing, discussing text, and reading instruction.* This combination helps English learners relate their background experiences to text (Saunders & Goldenberg, 1999).

4. *Develop the concepts necessary for comprehension.* Because English learners bring to school many different experiences and concepts, it is important to develop key concepts before asking children to read.

5. *Preview text, teach key words, and have children follow along as you read aloud.* Comprehension improves when teachers combine previewing with teaching key words and have English learners follow along as the teacher reads aloud (O'Donnell, Weber, & McLaughlin, 2003).

3. Compile all the scenes or events. Have children suggest the proper order.

4. Call on volunteers to explain each scene or event.

5. Ask children to close their eyes while you remove a scene or event. Place all scenes (or social studies events) side-by-side. Ask children to tell which scene (or event) is missing. (You may want to tape scenes to the board in this step.)

6. After discussing the pictures, have the groups write a short description of the action depicted in the pictures they drew.

## 6.12    Story Maps, Organizers, and Frames

- Large group, small group, pairs, or individual
- Use for identifying story structure.

Story maps, organizers, and frames are graphic displays that help children understand the elements of a story and the events in a story they have read.

**Material:** A copy of a story for each child; a story map, organizer, or frame for each child.

**Step-by-step directions:**

### Story Maps

Maps are most effective for beginning readers who have not had many experiences with stories prior to coming to school and for less able readers (Boulineau, Fore, III, Hagan-Burke, & Burke, 2004).

1. Introduce the elements of the story by reading a story aloud while the children follow along in the text. Stop at key points to discuss the setting, characters, problem, solution, and other story elements. Model how to use story structure to guide story reading.

2. Give each child a map for the story (Figure 6–8). Complete the story map as a whole-group activity. Discuss the story elements.

3. When children have developed some familiarity with story structure, have them work with a partner to complete story maps (Figure 6–8).

### Story Organizers

Story organizers are appropriate for first, second, and third graders who need practice thinking about story structure.

1. Demonstrate how to use the story organizer to write a brief version of a familiar story.

2. Have children complete the organizer (Figure 6–9).

3. Share the finished organizers; talk about the story elements; discuss how the completed organizers children wrote differ in content but not in organization.

### Story Frames

These are suitable for children who have a sense of story structure.

**Figure 6–8**
Story Map
Showing Story
Elements

---

**SETTING**

Characters _____   _____   _____

_____   _____   _____

**PROBLEM**

Attempts to solve the problem

Event 1. _____

Event 2. _____

Event 3. _____

**HOW THE PROBLEM IS SOLVED**

**HOW THE CHARACTERS REACT OR FEEL**

---

**Figure 6–9**
Story Organizer

SOMEBODY _____ (fill in the WHO and DETAILS)

WANTED _____

BUT _____

SO _____

For the Three Little Pigs the organizer might look like this: The hungry wolf WANTED to eat a pig for dinner BUT the wolf couldn't get into the third little pig's brick house SO the wolf went away and ate three fish he caught in the river instead.

1. Introduce a story frame by retelling a familiar story or reading a short story to the group. Model how to use the story frame to reflect on and react to the story (Figure 6–10).

2. Once children are familiar with story frames, have everyone in the group read the same story. After reading, ask pairs to complete a story frame.

**Figure 6–10**
Story Frame

Title _____

Author _____

## SETTING FRAME

The setting for the story is _____.
<br>(where and when)

I think the story took place in _____ because _____
_____. I think the story took place _____
<br>(where)                                                      (when)

because the story said _____
_____.

The most important character in this story is _____. I think _____
<br>(name)                                      (main character)

was_____ because the story said _____.
<br>(trait or feeling)

## PLOT FRAME

_____ wanted to _____.
<br>(main character)                              (goal)
_____.

I can tell that _____ wanted to _____
the story said _____
_____.

The first thing _____ tried was to _____
<br>(main character)
_____.
<br>(what the character did to reach the goal)

_____ was not successful because the story said
<br>(main character)
that _____.

The second thing _____ tried was _____
<br>(main character)
_____.

I could tell that _____ was successful because the
<br>(main character)
story said that _____.

## RESOLUTION FRAME

The story ended when _____
_____.

I think _____ was _____
<br>(main character)                  (how the character felt)

because the story said that _____
_____.

My Reaction

I _____ this story because _____
<br>(how you feel about the story)
_____.

Another Ending: Another way to end this story is for _____
_____

3. In discussing the completed story frames, help children understand that responses should be logical and each response should be linked to previous responses. Also stress that there is not one right answer to some parts of the story frame. Talk about differences in children's perceptions and interpretations.

---

## 6.13    Sticky Note Self-Monitoring

- Small group or individual
- Use for self-monitoring.

Sticky notes are a useful tool to encourage self-monitoring.

**Material:** Several sticky notes for each child; text for each child.

**Step-by-step directions:**

1. Discuss prompts that encourage self-monitoring. Write prompts on the board.
2. Give children sticky notes. Have them write one prompt on each sticky note. Model how to use the sticky note prompts to monitor comprehension.
3. Children read a short selection and place sticky notes with questions in strategic places throughout the text. Phrase prompts in the first person.

   Ideas for Sticky Note Prompts

   Do I understand this?

   What is the main point I should remember?

   What does this mean?

   Does this fit with what I already know?

   Why did this happen?

   Customize prompts for the text and the children whom you teach.

4. Encourage children to add their own sticky note questions while reading. After reading, talk about the sticky note questions and ask children to explain how they found information.

---

## 6.14    Sticky Note Click and Clunk

- Small group, pairs, or individual
- Use for self-monitoring.

Click and clunk encourages readers to reflect on their own comprehension and gives them an easy-to-remember mnemonic to activate self-monitoring (Vaughn & Klingner, 1999). Reading clicks when the child understands text. Reading clunks when the child does not understand the text or cannot figure out a word.

**Material:** A copy of the text for each child; sticky notes; pencils.

**Step-by-step directions:**

1. Explain that clicks happen when we understand meaning, clunks when we do not comprehend or do not know a word.

2. Have children read a short selection. Ask them to be on the lookout for clunks. Have children raise their hands when reading clunks. Discuss the clunks as they occur.

3. Once children are familiar with click and clunk, have them read another selection and put a sticky note in the margin beside each clunk. Children make a small notation on each sticky note telling about the clunk. They write an M for a meaning clunk and a W for a word clunk.

4. After reading, ask children to describe the sticky note clunks. Discuss the clunks with the whole group; talk about ways to fix the clunks. (Use whole-group discussions of the clunks the first few times children use this self-monitoring strategy.)

## 6.15    Story Impressions

- Large group, small group, pairs, or individual
- Use for making predictions.

Children use fragments of an unread story to predict events, and then compare their predictions with the story content (McGinley & Denner, 1987). Story impressions improves comprehension (Denner, McGinley, & Brown, 2001; Denner, Rickards, & Albanese, 2003).

**Material:** 10 to 15 words or phrases from an unread story; copies of the story for every child.

**Step-by-step instructions:**

1. Select 10 to 15 words or phrases from a story. Words and phrases should describe the characters, setting, and key plot elements, including the resolution.

2. Write on the board the words and phrases in the order in which they appear in the story.

3. Have the group use the words and phrases to predict story events. Ask children to suggest events using the words in the order in which they appear.

**Figure 6–11**
Story Impressions
for *The Story
About Ping*

Ping the duck
Yangtze river
Wise-eyed boat
Hunt for food
Late
Spank
Alone
Crumbs
Houseboat
Small boy
Duck dinner
Basket
Into the water
Spank
Home again

*From: The Story About Ping* by M. Flack, and K. Wiese, 1977, New York: Puffin Books.

4. Have children read the story. After reading, children compare and contrast the group's story with the story the author wrote.

5. Children may edit their story if they wish.

6. Another option is to have pairs or individuals use the key words to write stories. This option is most effective when children have participated in a group-written story experience with story impressions. Figure 6–11 is an example of a list of story impression words and phrases for *The Story About Ping* (Flack & Wiese, 1977).

## 6.16    QAR: Question-Answer-Relationship

- Large group, small group, pairs, or individual
- Use for identifying important facts, understanding relationships, making inferences, and judging text.

Use QAR—Question-Answer-Relationship—to guide children in locating answers to four types of questions: (1) *Right there* questions ask for literal information that is stated word-for-word in the text; (2) *Think and search* questions ask for information in different parts of the text and may call for inferences; (3) *Author and You* questions ask for inferences based on students' personal experience and information in the text; and (4) *On Your Own* questions are related to the topic, but ask students to use prior knowledge to judge text (Raphael, 1984; 1986).

**Materials:** Text for each child.

**Step-by-step directions:**

1. Make a chart showing the four types of questions. Explain the four types of questions. Read several short selections. Write one question for Right There, Think and Search, Author and Me, and On My Own on the board. Discuss where to find the answers in the selections.

2. Guide readers as they learn to identify Right There, Think and Search, Author and Me, and On My Own questions. Model how to answer questions and give readers practice answering questions under your guidance. Figure 6–12 shows QAR questions for Little Red Riding Hood.

3. When children are comfortable answering questions, have pairs write questions for two or more of the QAR categories, depending on children's development

**Figure 6–12**
QAR Questions for Hansel and Gretel

| *Right There* | What happened to the bread crumbs the children left in the woods? |
|---|---|
| | I can point to the answer in the story. |
| *Think and Search* | Why did Hansel stick a chicken bone out of the stall? |
| I must think about how the ideas in the story relate to one another. | |
| *Author and You* | What else might Gretel have done to help her brother? |
| I must think about what I read and my own ideas to answer this question. | |
| *On Your Own* | How would this story be different if the woman had been friendly? |
| I have to think about my own experiences to answer this question. | |

as readers. Ask children to share the questions they write. Discuss how to use the QAR questions to improve comprehension.

4. Encourage children to use QAR as they read. Review and revisit QAR as needed.

## INFORMAL ASSESSMENT OR ADDITIONAL PRACTICES FOR OBSERVING AND DEVELOPING COMPREHENSION

### Additional Practices

*Directed Reading-Thinking Activity (DRTA).* DRTA is particularly helpful in developing comprehension because children are actively involved in lessons. DRTA consists of before, during, and after reading activities. Before reading, children relate background knowledge to text, set purposes, and make predictions. Children read to verify or reject predictions, discuss text, and reread for different purposes, to clarify misconceptions, or to develop more in-depth comprehension. After reading, the children continue to develop strategies and concepts. DRTA lessons are most effective when children have enough background knowledge to make solid predictions and do not need a great deal of teacher guidance.

*Guided reading.* Guided reading is a lesson framework that develops strategies within the context of small, flexible groups of children who read text on a level appropriate for instruction. Teachers who use guided reading begin by selecting text on the instructional reading level of a small group and thinking of how to focus instruction on the type of text, and the particular needs of the children in the group. The teacher prepares the group to read by teaching key words, helping children relate their background knowledge to text, clarifying concepts, and introducing the title, author, and other book features. During reading, the teacher observes and assists children as they apply strategies. Teachers also note the reading ability and strategy application of individuals in the small group. After reading, the children discuss the text. Follow-up includes a range of activities, depending on the needs of the children in the group. Generally speaking, guided reading is used by first-, second-, and third-grade teachers.

*Think-aloud.* Thinking aloud is talking through the thought process. Readers think aloud when they explain their thoughts and strategies while reading. This gives children a model to follow and insight into strategy use and problem solving. There are three ways you might use think-alouds:

1. *Teacher think-alouds.* Share your thoughts as you read text. Explain how, why, and when you use different reading strategies. Sum up the strategies you used and why you used them. For example, you might demonstrate how to make inferences by stopping at logical points to ask inferential questions and determine important and not-so-important information. Model answering inferential questions and conclude by recapping your thought processes.

2. *Reader think-alouds.* Encourage readers to stop at key points in a selection and to talk about the strategies they are using and what they have learned so far, make inferences, and set purposes for further reading. Research shows that thinking aloud while reading results in more inferences than reading without thinking aloud (Liang & Kamhi, 2002).

3. *Write think-alouds.* Have children write their thoughts as they read (Oster, 2001). This approach, according to Oster, results in greater class participation

and improved comprehension. Written think-alouds reveal readers' strengths, as well as prior knowledge, misunderstood information, and misinterpretations. Children share and discuss their written think-alouds with a partner or small groups or write think-alouds on the board and then discuss them in a large group in an atmosphere of respect for others' views.

*K-W-L.* The K-W-L teaching technique (Ogle, 1986) asks children to list what they know about a topic (K), what they would like to know (W), and write what they learned (L) after reading. KWL helps children connect their background knowledge to text, set purposes, develop vocabulary, and reflect on text.

*PowerPoint.* Have children create their own PowerPoint presentations. Children might, for example, make a presentation that describes a character, lists the sequence of events, or retells a familiar story from another point of view. PowerPoint helps readers organize thinking, reflect on text, and make connections with text, to mention just a few benefits.

*Developing the main idea.* Alternative ways for children to state the main idea include: (a) sketching the main idea, (b) making bumper stickers or decals that state the main idea, (c) writing captions for pictures and ads, (d) writing subtitles for each paragraph in a content-subject textbook, or (e) matching titles with newspaper or magazine articles.

*Cause-and-effect clue words.* Children need to identify cause-and-effect relationships in order to make inferences. Teach children to be on the lookout for words that are clues to cause-and-effect relationships.

## Informal Assessment in the Classroom

Observations give us insight into whether children comprehend text well enough to succeed in the classroom. If you observe the same level of comprehension in literature groups or guided reading, during social studies and science, and while the child reads library books, you can be assured that you have captured a true picture of the child's ability. If you wish to get more specific information, you will need to structure observations. There are three classroom-friendly alternatives: informal reading inventories, retelling, and cloze.

*Informal reading inventories.* Informal reading inventories (IRIs) include short passages for oral and silent reading. These inventories indicate the level of text that is easy, just right for instruction, or too difficult for the child. Examples of informal reading inventories include: (1) Classroom Reading Inventory (Silvaroli & Wheelock, 2004), (2) Analytical Reading Inventory (Woods & Moe, 2007) and (3) Ekwall/Shanker Reading Inventory (Ekwall & Shanker, 2000).

*Retelling.* The child reads a text and then recounts what he or she remembers. We learn (1) what the child thinks is important about the text and (2) whether the structure and/or sequence of the retelling matches the text. By third grade, children should include the setting, a main idea, supporting details, the problem, events in sequence, and a conclusion. Inferences and generalizations beyond the story itself are also important. When the child cannot remember further detail, the teacher uses questions to prompt memory. For example, the teacher might ask, "Tell me more about

_____" or "Can you remember anything else about _____."
Figure 6–13 is an example of a retelling guide for a simple story.

English language learners may fully understand a story but be unable to spontaneously retell the story. Likewise, children who have mild difficulty using spoken language to express themselves may struggle with retelling. Offer more support to these children. If spontaneous retelling is sketchy, use questions to prompt the child. If the English learner or the child with a mild spoken language disability retells quite well with prompts, then you can assume that the child understands the story.

*Cloze.* Cloze passages have words deleted and replaced by a blank. Children use reading vocabulary, context clues, and background knowledge to identify the missing word. Cloze is better suited to children in third through sixth grades. Cloze passages may be used to identify independent, instructional, and frustration levels. Follow these steps to construct your own cloze passages:

1. Select a 300-word passage appropriate for the grade you teach.
2. The passage should make sense outside the context of the surrounding text.
3. Leave the first and last sentences intact.
4. Beginning with the second sentence, delete every fifth word and replace it with a blank to produce fifty blanks. All blanks should be the same length.

**Figure 6–13**
Retelling Guide
for a Simple Story

Story _____

Level _____

Date _____

|  | Unprompted | Prompted |
|---|---|---|
| Setting |  |  |
| • Place |  |  |
| • Time |  |  |
| • Characters |  |  |
| • Character traits |  |  |
| Problem |  |  |
| • Describes the problem |  |  |
| Solution |  |  |
| • Describes attempts to solve the problem |  |  |
| Sequence |  |  |
| • Recalls the correct sequence of events |  |  |
| Text Language |  |  |
| • Uses words from the text |  |  |
| • Uses phrases repeated in the text |  |  |
| Connects the Story to: |  |  |
| • Own life experiences |  |  |
| • Expresses an opinion of the story |  |  |
| • Expresses an opinion of the author or illustrator |  |  |

**Prompt:** Tell me more about _____.

What else can you remember about _____?

Children read the passage silently. There are 50 points possible—one for each blank—and only exact replacements count. Spelling does not affect the score. The percent of correct replacements indicates whether the text is appropriate for independent reading, instruction, or is too difficult. Doubling the number of correct replacements yields the percent correct. The percentages associated with each level are as follows:

Independent level ranges from 57% to 100% correct.
Instructional level is from 44% to 56% correct.
Frustration level falls below 43% correct.

These percentages were established by counting only exact replacements. If you count synonyms, these percentages cannot be used to determine the child's reading ability.

## COMPREHENSION IN THE CLASSROOM

All classroom reading programs emphasize comprehension. The main difference among programs is the level of thinking and the specific comprehension strategies children learn.

### Kindergarten

Kindergarten teachers teach story structure to kindergartners who have not already developed this knowledge. Kindergartners learn to identify the setting and important events, retell stories, and act out important story events. Comprehension is taught when the teacher reads story and information books aloud. As teachers read aloud they model fluent reading, ask questions to encourage children to relate the story to their own lives, engage children to set purposes for listening, and show kindergartners how to locate the author and illustrator. Kindergartners who can read easy books learn to use picture clues and text to understand stories, predict events, set purposes, and monitor their own comprehension.

### First Grade

First graders learn to follow one- or two-step directions and use context to work out word identification and sentence meaning. Children also learn to answer who, what, where, when, and how questions. They develop comprehension through reading simple stories and information text and through direct instruction. First-grade teachers teach children to identify important ideas, distinguish fantasy from realistic text, make and confirm predictions, identify cause-effect relationships, state the main idea, and draw conclusions. First graders develop the strategy of monitoring their own reading and learn fix-up strategies to resolve misunderstandings. First-grade classroom reading programs also include teaching children to resolve ambiguities in meaning by (1) interpreting picture clues, (2) looking back to find information, (3) rereading, (4) using context clues, and (5) asking for help.

### Second Grade

Second graders learn to use titles, tables of contents, and chapter headings to find ideas in information text. Children learn to ask why, what-if, and how questions; state their purposes for reading; and follow two-step directions. Second graders begin to develop the strategies of comparing and contrasting facts in information books and comparing and contrasting plots, settings, and characters in stories from around the world. Second graders also learn to summarize short text; interpret simple diagrams, charts, and graphs; and create mental images from descriptions in stories and poems.

## Third Grade

Third grade is a transition year. During this year the classroom reading program shifts away from teaching the basics to teaching children to use reading to learn new information. Third graders learn to support their answers with a combination of information from the text and prior knowledge and to make simple maps, graphs, and charts. Third-grade teachers teach children how to follow multiple-step directions, differentiate fact from opinion, restate facts and details, and identify the speaker or narrator. The third-grade classroom program continues to develop the strategies of answering specific questions, including how, why, and what-if questions; identifying problems and solutions; and summarizing text. Third graders are also introduced to the strategy of using information in text to modify predictions.

## Fourth Grade

Fourth-grade classroom reading programs are markedly different from earlier programs. Children read a variety of information text, including subject-matter textbooks, reference material, and online text. Children learn to follow multiple-step directions in a basic technical manual such as those for computer commands and video games. The fourth-grade program includes teaching children how to find information, compare different sources, identify implied main ideas, make inferences, draw conclusions, recognize text intended to persuade and evaluate the author's purpose. Fourth graders also learn to compare and contrast plots, settings, and characters and generate credible alternative endings for story text.

### WORKING WITH CHILDREN AT RISK

1. *Use more teacher-directed instruction.* Children at risk develop comprehension at a faster rate when their teachers use teacher-directed instruction—designing learning experiences, monitoring learning, and identifying outcomes and products—than when children take the lead in selecting and monitoring learning experiences (Conner, Morrison, & Petrella, 2004; Williams, 2005).

2. *Encourage and develop self-monitoring.* Learning to self-monitor helps struggling readers keep track of meaning, and this, in turn, improves comprehension (Oakhill, Hartt, & Samols, 2005).

3. *Provide high-quality supplemental instruction.* Comprehension improves when children receive high-quality, carefully crafted instruction in addition to normal classroom instruction (McIntyre, et al., 2005).

4. *Preteach words that are necessary for comprehension (National Reading Panel, 2000).* Preteaching the meaning of important words improves comprehension and results in better fluency (Burns, Dean, & Foley, 2004).

5. *Teach story structure.* Knowing the structure of stories helps children organize their thinking, facilitates remembering information, and improves comprehension (Boulineau, Fore, III, Hagan-Burke, & Burke, 2005; Williams, 2005).

6. *Adjust text difficulty to children's reading development.* Use instructional-level text to teach reading and offer children a wide selection of independent-level text to read for pleasure (Ivey, 2002).

7. *Combine repeated reading with having children ask questions during reading.* Rereading text and asking questions about meaning improves fluency and the ability to make inferences (Therrien, Wickstrom, & Jones, 2006).

## Fifth Grade

Fifth graders continue to refine and polish the strategies developed in the fourth grade. Fifth-graders learn to identify the structure of various forms of text, including magazines and online text. Fifth-grade teachers teach children to identify facts and evidence that support ideas, infer ideas and sequence, evaluate information, and interpret character traits, actions, and motives. Children also learn to recognize stated and implied themes, identify underlying themes, and describe the function and effect of common literary devices such as imagery, metaphor, and symbolism.

## Sixth Grade

Sixth-grade classroom reading programs extend the strategies and abilities taught in the fifth grade. Sixth graders read more varied text, learn to take notes, identify the structural features of popular media, and interpret relationships. Sixth-grade teachers teach children how make reasonable statements about the text by citing outside sources and how to follow multistep directions for completing applications. Children become aware of unsupported information, faulty reasoning, and propaganda. Sixth-grade programs also include teaching children to critique the plot, identify forms of fiction, analyze the effect of the setting on the problem and resolution, explain the effects of literary devices, and recognize the difference between first and third person. By the end of sixth grade, children are adept at reading information and story text, skilled at using reading as a learning tool, and are developing the ability to critically evaluate text.

# REFERENCES

Bimmel, P. (2001). Effects of reading strategy introduction in secondary education—A review of intervention studies. *Educational Studies in Language and Literature, 1,* 273–298.

Boulineau, T., Fore, C., III, Hagan-Burke, S., & Burke, M. D. (2004). Use of story-mapping to increase the story-grammar text comprehension of elementary students with learning disabilities. *Learning Disability Quarterly, 27,* 105–121.

Brandão, A. C. P., & Oakhill, J. (2005). "How do you know this answer?" Children's use of text data and general knowledge in story comprehension. *Reading and Writing, 18,* 687–713.

Burns, M. K., Dean, V. J., & Foley, S. (2004). Preteaching unknown key words with incremental rehearsal to improve reading fluency and comprehension with children identified as reading disabled. *Journal of School Psychology, 42,* 303–314.

Carlisle, J. F., & Beeman, M. M. (2000). The effects of language of instruction on reading and writing achievement of first-grade Hispanic children. *Scientific Studies of Reading, 4,* 331–353.

Chapman, J. W., & Tunmer, W. E. (2003). Reading difficulties, reading-related self-perceptions, and strategies for overcoming negative self-beliefs. *Reading & Writing Quarterly, 19,* 5–24.

Chard, D. J., Pikulski, J. J., & McDonagh, S. H. (2006). Fluency: The link between decoding and comprehension of struggling readers. In T. Rasinksi, C. Blachowica, & K. Lems (Eds.), *Fluency instruction: Research-based best practices* (pp. 39–61). New York: Guilford Press.

Connor, C., M. D., Morrison, F. J., & Petrella, J. N. (2004). Effective reading comprehension instruction: Examining child × instruction interaction. *Journal of Educational Psychology, 96,* 682–698.

Denner, P. R., McGinley, W. J., & Brown, E. (2001). Effects of story impressions as a rereading/writing story on story comprehension. *Journal of Educational Research, 82,* 329–336.

Denner, P. R., Rickards, J. P., & Albanese, A. J. (2003). The effect of story impressions preview on learning from narrative text. *The Journal of Experimental Education, 71,* 313–332.

Ekwall, E. E., & Shanker, J. L. (2000). *Ekwall/Shanker reading inventory* (4th ed.). Boston: Allyn and Bacon.

Flack, M. & Wiese, K. (1977). *The Story About Ping.* Grosset & Dunlap, NY: NY.

Glenberg, A. M., Gutierrez, T., Levin, J. R., Japuntich, S., & Kaschak, M. P. (2004). Activity and imagined activity can enhance young children's reading comprehension. *Journal of Educational Psychology, 96*, 424–436.

Hall, K. M., Sabey, B. L., & McClellan, M. (2005). Expository text comprehension: Helping primary-grade teachers use expository texts to full advantage. *Reading Psychology, 26*, 211–234.

Harmon, J. M., Hedrick, W. B., & Wood, K. D. (2005). Research on vocabulary instruction in the content areas: Implications for struggling readers. *Reading and Writing Quarterly, 21*, 261–280.

Hutchinson, J. M., Whiteley, H. E., Smith, C. D., & Connors, L. (2003). The developmental progression of comprehension-related skills in children learning EAL. *Journal of Research in Reading, 26*, 19–32.

Ivey, G. (2002). Building comprehension when they're still learning to read the words. In C. C. Block & M. Pressley (Eds.), *Comprehension instruction: Research-based best practices* (pp. 234–246). Baltimore, MD: Guilford Press.

Joshi, H. M. (2005). Vocabulary: A critical component of comprehension. *Reading and Writing Quarterly, 21*, 209–219.

Manzo, A. V. (1969). The ReQuest procedure. *Journal of Reading, 2*, 123–126.

McGinley, W., & Denner, P. (1987). Story impressions: A prereading/writing strategy. *Journal of Reading, 31*, 248–253.

McKenzie, G. R., & Danielson, E. (2003). Improving comprehension through mural lessons. *The Reading Teacher, 56*, 739–742.

McIntyre, E., et al. (2005). Supplemental instruction in early reading: Does it matter for struggling readers? *Journal of Educational Research, 99*, 99–107.

Miller, J. F., Heilmann, J., Nockerts, A., Iglesias, A., & Fabiano, L. (2006). Oral language and reading in bilingual children. *Learning Disabilities Research & Practice, 21*, 30–43.

National Reading Panel (2000). *Report of the national reading panel. Teaching children to read: An evidence-based assessment of the scientific research literature on reading and its implications for reading instruction: Reports of the subgroups* (NIH Publication No. 00-4754). Washington, DC: U.S. Government Printing Office.

Oakhill, J., Hartt, J., & Samols, D. (2005). Levels of comprehension monitoring and working memory in good and poor comprehenders. *Reading and Writing, 18*, 657–686.

O'Donnell, P., Weber, K. P., & McLaughlin, T. F. (2003). Improving correct and error rate and reading comprehension using key words and previewing: A case report with a language minority student. *Education and Treatment of Children, 26*, 237–254.

Ogle, D. M. (1986). K-W-L: A teaching model that develops active reading of expository text. *The Reading Teacher, 39*, 564–570.

Oster, L. (2001). Using the think-aloud for reading instruction. *The Reading Teacher, 55*, 64–69.

Proctor, C. P., Carlo, M. S., August, D., & Snow, C. (2006). The intriguing role of Spanish language vocabulary knowledge in predicting English reading comprehension. *Journal of Educational Psychology, 98*, 159–169.

Raphael, T. E. (1984). Teaching learners about sources of information for answering questions. *The Reading Teacher, 28*, 303–311.

Raphael, T. E. (1986). Teaching question-answer relationships: revisited. *Journal of Reading, 27*, 301–311.

Saunders, W. M., & Goldenberg, C. (1999). Effects of instructional conversation and literature logs on limited- and fluent-English proficient students' story comprehension and thematic understanding. *The Elementary School Journal, 99*, 279–301.

Silvaroli, N. J., & Wheelock, W. H. (2004). *Classroom reading inventory* (10th ed.). New York: McGraw-Hill.

Therrien, W. J., Wickstrom, K., & Jones, K. (2006). Effect of combined repeated readings and questions generation on reading achievement. *Learning Disabilities Research and Practice, 21*, 89–97.

Thiede, K. W., & Anderson, M. C. M. (2003). Summarizing can improve metacomprehension accuracy. *Contemporary Educational Psychology, 28*, 129–160.

Trabasso, T., & Bouchard, E. (2002). Teaching readers how to comprehend text strategically. In C. C. Block & M. Pressley (Eds.), *Comprehension instruction: Research-based best practices* (pp. 176–200). Baltimore, MD: Guilford Press.

Vaughn, S., & Klingner, J. K. (1999). Teaching reading comprehension through collaborative strategic reading. *Intervention in School & Clinic, 34*, 284–292.

Williams, J. P. (2005). Instruction in reading comprehension for primary grade students: A focus on text structure. *The Journal of Special Education, 39*, 6–18.

Williams, J. P., Hall, K. M., Lauer, K. D., Stafford, L. K. B, & deCani, J. S. (2005). Expository text comprehension in the primary grade classroom. *Journal of Educational Psychology, 97*, 538–550.

Woods, M. L., & Moe, A. J. (2007). *Analytical reading inventory* (8th ed.). Upper Saddle River, NJ: Pearson Merrill Prentice Hall.

Zinar, S. (2005). "How do you know this answer?"—Children's use of text data and general knowledge in story comprehension. *Reading and Writing, 18*, 687–713.